Eyewitness
ARCTIC & ANTARCTIC

Arctic plant

Net for catching ptarmigan

Reindeer-skin winter coat from Siberia

Siberian shaman's staff

Antarctic explorer's compass

Siberian ivory model of reindeer drawing a sled

Northern
fleabane
plant

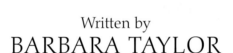

Snowshoe
for a pony

Eyewitness
ARCTIC &
ANTARCTIC

Written by
BARBARA TAYLOR

Photographed by
GEOFF BRIGHTLING

Carving of polar
bear from Canada

DK Publishing

Model of Greenland canoe

Engraved ivory

Cribbage board
made from
walrus tusk

DK

**LONDON, NEW YORK,
MELBOURNE, MUNICH, AND DELHI**

Project editor Gillian Denton
Art editor Jane Tetzlaff
Managing editor Simon Adams
Managing art editor Julia Harris
Researcher Céline Carez
Editorial Assistance Djinn von Noorden, David Pickering
Production Catherine Semark
Picture research Clive Webster

REVISED EDITION

Revised by Richard Beatty & John Woodward

DK INDIA
Project editor Nidhi Sharma
Project art editor Rajnish Kashyap
Editor Pallavi Singh
Designer Mahipal Singh
Deputy managing editor Eman Chowdhary
Managing art editor Romi Chakraborty
DTP designer Tarun Sharma
Picture researcher Sumedha Chopra

DK UK
Senior editor Rob Houston
Senior art editor Philip Letsu
Production editor Tony Phipps
Publisher Andrew Macintyre

First published in the United States in 1995
by DK Publishing, 375 Hudson Street, New York, New York 10014

10 9 8 7 6 5 4 3 2 1

001—183544—Jan/12

DK books are available at special discounts when purchased in
bulk for sales promotions, premiums, fundraising, or educational use.
For details, contact: DK Publishing Special Markets
375 Hudson Street, New York, New York 10014
SpecialSales@dk.com
A catalog record for this book is available
from the Library of Congress.

ISBN: 978-0-7566-9071-7 (Hardback)
978-0-7566-9072-4 (Library binding)

Color reproduction by
Colourscan, Singapore
Printed and bound in China
by Toppan Printing Co.
(Shenzhen) Ltd.

Discover more at
www.dk.com

Shaman's
eagle from
Siberia

Siberian shaman's apron

Both the Arctic
and Antarctic support
some plant life

Husky dogs

Contents

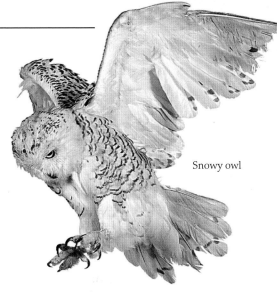

Snowy owl

The ends of the Earth

THE TWO POLAR REGIONS at the very ends of the Earth are among the coldest, windiest, and most remote places on the planet. A huge, frozen ocean—the Arctic—surrounds the North Pole; while a vast area of frozen land—Antarctica— surrounds the South Pole (see maps on pp. 64–65). Both the Arctic and Antarctic have long, dark, freezing winters. During the short summer, the Sun shines all the time and animals flock to the polar areas to feed and nest. The Arctic and Antarctic are the last two wilderness areas on Earth. However, the Arctic has already been exploited for its mineral wealth, and both polar regions are increasingly threatened by climate change (see pp. 66–67).

Arctic

Antarctic

The position of the Arctic and the Antarctic

TRAPPED BY THE ICE
In 1596, a Dutch explorer, William Barents, set off on his third attempt to find a route from Europe to China and India around the North Pole. When his ship was trapped by sea ice, he and his crew were forced to winter ashore, building a cabin from the wrecked ship. In the spring, the men set off for Europe in the ship's boats. Barents himself died, but his men survived.

A WHITE WORLD
Ice dominates the landscapes and seascapes of the polar regions— as seen here in the Antarctic Peninsula. This peninsula is the most accessible part of the Antarctic continent to visiting tourist ships. Here, a summer scene is shown, with the sea ice broken up into small fragments. Once winter comes, the ocean becomes completely frozen over again.

MYSTERY LAND

In the 4th century BCE, the Greek philosopher Aristotle suggested the existence of a southern landmass, known in latin as *Terra Australis Incognita*—the unknown southern continent. Mapmakers included a huge southern continent on their maps until 1773, but it was not until Captain James Cook's exploration in the mid-18th century that anyone knew what was really there.

NORTHERN LIGHTS

Auroras are wispy curtains of light that appear in the sky above the poles. They can sometimes take the form of brightly colored shooting rays. Auroras are caused by charged particles from the Sun striking gases in Earth's atmosphere above the poles. This makes the gases give off light.

MIDNIGHT SUN

In regions near the North and South poles, the Sun never sets for several months during the summer. This happens because of the tilt of the Earth toward the Sun. While one pole has constant daylight, the other is shrouded in winter darkness because the Sun never rises.

Land ice is built up from centuries of falling snow. It flows slowly downhill and may extend over the sea as an ice shelf hundreds of feet thick

Broken fragment of ice shelf—a vast iceberg

Sea ice is usually less than 16 ft (5 m) thick. This small fragment here is probably less than 3 ft (1 m) thick. Sea ice may be continuous, as it is over much of the Arctic Ocean, or in fragments

Small, melted fragment of iceberg

The Arctic and tundra

AT THE CENTER OF THE ARCTIC REGION is a vast area of permanently frozen ice floating on the Arctic Ocean. The Arctic region also includes the largest island in the world, Greenland, the island of Spitsbergen, and the northern edges of North America, Asia, and Europe. South of the Arctic Ocean is the tundra, which means "treeless plain" in Russian. The landscape is low and flat, with many lichens, mosses, grasses, and sprawling, low bushes. Trees cannot grow in the true Arctic because they are unable to stand up to the intense cold and fierce winter winds. The main sea connection of the Arctic Ocean is with the Atlantic, whose warmer waters push back the point at which the permanent ice exists.

Marshy pools form because permafrost prevents water from draining away

MAPPING THE COAST
In 1819–22, Sir John Franklin, who later lost his life searching for the elusive Northwest Passage (p. 52), made a hazardous land expedition charting the coast of Canada. At one point he took a canoe, which was particularly dangerous as the ice was breaking up. Wooden ships and boats of the 19th century could easily be crushed or trapped by ice.

The timberline, where forest gives way to tundra, is often taken to be the southern boundary of the true Arctic

Frozen layer, called permafrost, a little way below the surface

BEAR JOURNEYS
Polar bears live only in the Arctic. They make long journeys across the Arctic sea ice, hunting for seals. The bears are expert divers and swimmers and often hitch rides on ice floes. One polar bear was found swimming 200 miles (320 km) from land. Polar bears can also dive from the top of icebergs more than 50 ft (15 m) into the water.

Permanent sea ice lasting from year to year

SINKING THE UNSINKABLE
Icebergs are huge chunks of floating ice that originate from land glaciers and ice shelves. The most famous iceberg casualty was the *Titanic*, supposedly unsinkable, which was sunk on her maiden voyage in April 1912. The *Titanic's* iceberg, like others encountered in the North Atlantic, originated in Greenland.

Some sea ice melts and breaks up in the summer and refreezes in the winter—this is often called pack ice

Ice floes are drifting fragments of sea ice

At the edges of the ocean, ice forms in the winter and melts again in the summer

Only low-growing plants survive on the tundra

Summer in Denali National Park, Alaska

FROZEN PROBLEMS
A permanently frozen layer called permafrost occurs a little way below the surface of the Arctic soil. It can be up to about 3,000 ft (900 m) thick. The ground above the permafrost thaws in the summer and the water collects on the surface, forming lakes and marshes. Buildings and roads have to be specially insulated to avoid melting the permafrost, or they begin to collapse. Disposal of sewage, waste water, and garbage also damages the permafrost.

Loiseleuria procumbens, a member of the heather family, grows across the Arctic region

ARCTIC PLANTS
Arctic plants have adapted in various ways to the low Arctic temperatures and a short growing season. Some can photosynthesize (make their own food) at temperatures below freezing. The plants grow rapidly in the spring, taking advantage of the long periods of daylight. There are over 500 species of wildflowers, and in the summer, the Arctic is ablaze with color. Some grasses have vertical leaves to catch the low-angled sunlight.

The Antarctic

THE CONTINENT OF ANTARCTICA is twice the size of Australia and one and a half times the size of the United States. It is also three times higher than any other continent—almost all of it is covered by an ice sheet that is, on average, 8,000 ft (2,500 m) thick. This height is a major reason for the extreme cold in Antarctica. The average winter temperature is -76°F (-60°C). Antarctica's harsh climate and its isolation from other continents have greatly reduced the variety of its wildlife—the largest animal that lives on land all year round is a tiny insect. During the summer, however, many animals, including penguins, whales, and seals, visit the continent to take advantage of the rich food supply and safe breeding sites around the coasts. Plants are very sparse and consist mostly of lichens, mosses, and liverworts.

HARDY SURVIVOR
Among the few types of living thing able to grow on land in Antarctica are lichens. A lichen is a double organism, in which a fungus teams up with a simple plant (alga). Lichens are slow growing and can resist extreme conditions well.

WARMER CLIMATE
Antarctica was not always cold. Fossil ferns (above) provide evidence of a warmer, subtropical climate about 70 million years ago, even in polar regions. But the plants would still have experienced several months of darkness each year.

SOUTH POLE PENGUINS
Penguins live only in the Southern Hemisphere. In the Arctic, auks have a similar lifestyle to penguins. They also look like penguins, but auks can fly, and penguins cannot.

Only 10 percent of an iceberg is visible above water level

ICEBERGS
When snow falls on the Antarctic plateau, it turns into ice. The ice is compacted and flows down toward the coastal ice shelves, where it is broken up by ocean tides, currents, and waves. This is how icebergs form. Some icebergs are so large—up to 150 miles (240 km) long and 70 miles (110 km) wide—that they can be tracked by satellites for several years before they melt.

COILED CLUES
Swimming shellfish with coiled shells, called ammonites, were common in the warm seas of prehistoric times. The last ammonites died out about 65 million years ago, but fossil ammonites found on Antarctica show that Antarctic seas were warmer millions of years ago.

WEIGHT OF ICE
About 98 percent of Antarctica is covered by an immense ice sheet, which in some places is over 2.5 miles (4 km) thick. Most of the mountains, and all of the lower ground, are buried under ice. Only a few jagged peaks, called nunataks, stick out. The enormous weight of the ice pushes most of the rocky surface of Antarctica below sea level. The ice in the lowest layers of the ice sheet is thought to be at least 200,000 years old.

DRY VALLEYS
Hidden among the Transantarctic Mountains are vast dry valleys, which are bare of snow and ice for much of the year. The valleys originally dried out because the mountains held back the ice cap. Winds rushing down the valleys suck away any moisture, forming large areas of bare rock in the middle of the continent.

CLEARING THE ICE
Special ships called icebreakers are used to clear routes through frozen polar seas. Before icebreakers, many early polar explorers saw their fragile wooden ships crushed by the power of the ice. Icebreakers have a specially shaped bow and a reinforced hull. They push the bow on top of the ice until the weight of the ship breaks through it.

As icebergs melt, they often form fascinating shapes

The erosive forces of ocean and winds combine to carve the ice

Life in Antarctic waters

IN CONTRAST TO THE SMALL VARIETY of animals on the land, there is an incredible wealth of life in the sea around Antarctica. In shallow waters, ice scrapes against the seabed, preventing any life. But in deeper waters below the crust of ice, there is a greater variety of life in the Antarctic Ocean than in the Arctic Ocean. Corals and anemones are anchored to the seabed, along with some 300 varieties of sponges. Many sea creatures feed on each other or on plankton. Food is scarce for most of the year. The cold affects the life cycles of many inhabitants. Animals function more slowly. They produce fewer, larger eggs and care for them longer. Many animals live longer than their counterparts in warmer waters. Some sponges live for several centuries.

COMMON CREATURES
Antarctic squid (top) have no shell, which may be useful in icy waters, where shells grow very slowly. They seize prey in their two long tentacles. Some types of comb jelly (bottom) are also common predators in Antarctic waters.

DUAL-PURPOSE SPINES
Seabed animals such as the sea urchin *Sterechinus neumayer* may move to shallower water during the summer, when they are not in danger from ice scouring the rocks on which they live. Their dense covering of mobile spines is used for both movement and defense.

The spines of sea urchins are often poisonous

Point at the end of the leg to dig for food in the seabed

SEA LEGS
Orange sea spiders with 10 to 12 giant legs are found in deeper Antarctic waters. The species shown (*Decolopoda australis*) has a diameter of 6 in (15 cm). It feeds on sea anemones, and like other Antarctic sea creatures, it develops very slowly.

COLD GIANTS
Many of the Antarctic's bottom-living invertebrates (creatures without backbones) are giants, such as this giant isopod *Glyptonotus antarcticus*, a relative of the woodlouse. It fills the ecological niche occupied by crabs in other parts of the world. *Glyptonotus* grows up to 8 in (20 cm), about three times bigger than similar species elsewhere. Growth is slow in the cold waters. Slow-growing invertebrates reach larger sizes than faster-growing ones. *Glyptonotus* scavenges around the seabed and eats anything it can find.

As well as the main legs, the spider has several smaller, limblike structures

Fingerlike outgrowths of coral filter out small zooplankton drifting past

ON THE ROCKS
A rock face about 26 to 33 ft (8 to 10 m) below the surface of the water provides a good anchorage for sponges, bryozoans (sea mosses), and the long hanging stalks of the soft coral *Ascolepis*. Sponges and some corals are abundant at depths of up to 0.6 miles (1 km).

Tentacles contain stinging cells that paralyze prey

TERRIBLE TENTACLES
Sea anemones capture prey, such as small fish or starfish, in their tentacles. The tentacles then pass the prey into the central mouth opening, ready to be digested and absorbed into the body. Waste is also excreted through the mouth.

OLD STARS
The seabed around Antarctica is sometimes covered with colorful red starfish. Starfish locate their prey by smell and grasp it with rows of suckered tube feet on the underside of their arms. Antarctic starfish live long lives—one is known to have lived to the age of 39.

Tube feet for walking, digging, and grasping prey

Migrants and residents

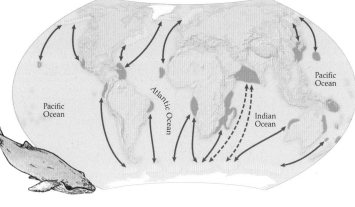

Migratory animals follow the sun

THE NUMBER AND VARIETY of animals living near the poles change dramatically with the seasons. Thousands of birds and mammals visit the Arctic or Antarctic only during the brief, light summer months, when it is relatively warm and there is plenty of food available. In addition to the food supply, advantages for summer migrants include safe places to rear their young, few predators, and a lack of competition for food and nesting spots. Often, the same traditional migration routes are used each year, but the animals also navigate using the positions of the Sun, Moon, and stars, Earth's magnetic field, and familiar landmarks. Journeys are often very dangerous, and many animals are killed before reaching their destination by bad weather, lack of food, and predators. Only a few hardy animals, such as the muskox, manage to stay in polar regions all year round.

Dense down feathers help to keep the geese warm

The bird save ene by flying V-forma the slips of the or in front

Thick skull and solid, horny band protect the brain when males clash horns

Muskox
Ovibos moschatus

Pacific Ocean

Pacific Ocean

Atlantic Ocean

Indian Ocean

← Main migration

◄---- Possible migration

Major feeding areas (summer)

Major feeding areas (winter)

FOOD IN THE FREEZER
Humpback whales in both the Northern and the Southern hemispheres travel to cold polar waters in the summer to take advantage of the rich food supply of plankton and fish. In the winter, when the sea freezes over, they migrate back to warmer tropical waters again to breed. They eat little during their tropical stopover, relying on their immense supply of body fat, built up during the summer.

Efficient wings allow the tern to cover up to 25,000 miles (40,000 km) on each round trip

Very long outer fur retains body warmth and keeps animal dry

CHAMPION TRAVELER
The graceful Arctic tern may see more daylight each year than any other creature. It breeds in large colonies during the Arctic summer. Then it flies all the way to the Antarctic to take advantage of the almost constant daylight and rich food supply of the Antarctic summer.

Arctic tern
Sterna paradisaea

MIGHTY MUSKOX
Tough, hardy muskoxen roam over the harsh tundra in herds made up of females and young, led by one or more strong bulls. In the summer, herds number about ten animals, but in the winter, muskoxen move south, in herds of 50 or more, wherever they can find food under the snow. Their name comes from the smell given off by the males during the breeding season.

The male's antlers are larger and thicker than those of the females

Caribou
Rangifer tarandus

FLIGHT OF THE SNOW GEESE
Many thousands of pairs of snow geese nest in the Arctic tundra in the summer. They migrate all the way from the Gulf of Mexico, a journey of about 2,000 miles (3,200 km). On their journey, they fly in flocks of tens of thousands of birds. The shorter days at the end of the summer tell the snow geese it is time to fly south once more.

SUMMER HOLIDAYS
Caribou herds are always on the move, wandering between their winter and summer feeding grounds and snatching bites of food wherever they can find it. In the spring, immense herds trek northward to feed on lichens and other low-growing tundra plants. They use well-marked trails that are often centuries old. As winter closes in, the caribou move south once more to the shelter of the forests.

Feet are tucked back during flight to make a more streamlined shape

Snow goose
Anser caerulescens

Curved horns used to defend against predators such as wolves

Dense, woolly underfur and thick layers of fat under the skin keep the muskox warm

Short, very strong legs support the massive body

Edges of hooves are sharp enough to dig through thick snow or ice to reach mosses, lichens, and roots underneath

Adaptable animals

To survive the contrasting seasons, animals have to act. As winter approaches, some mammals' fur coats grow thick. Winter fur is often white, which helps camouflage the animal against snow. A thick layer of fat in their skin traps extra warmth and acts as a food store in lean times. Birds also have layers of fat and dense, fluffy feathers, which keep out the cold. For many birds and mammals, the severe winter weather is just too much to cope with. They migrate south to warmer places, returning again in the spring. Insects lay their eggs in the warmer soil, and the larvae can withstand the freezing temperatures of the winter. As summer arrives, birds and mammals shed their thick coats. Animals that turn white in the winter often have brown summer camouflage.

FINE FURS
People in cold countries wear fur hats to stay warm through the coldest winters. They usually obtain them by snaring their original owners in traps.

Arctic fox
Alopex lagopus

DRESSED FOR SUMMER
In the summer, the Arctic fox grows a thinner coat of brownish-gray fur over most of its body. These colors match the brownish-gray rocks of the tundra landscape, making the fox hard to see so that it can creep up on its prey, such as lemmings, without being spotted. The fox stores food under rocks during the summer and comes back to eat it in the winter months when food is hard to find. Arctic foxes have a varied diet—they eat anything from berries, shells, and dead animals to garbage and birds and their eggs.

The chest and belly are usually a pale grayish-white

Short legs (and tail) lose less heat than long ones, as there is less surface area exposed to the air

Thick, bushy tail can be curled around the body for warmth during blizzards or when resting or sleeping

Antarctic ice fish
Chaenocephalus aceratus

ANTIFREEZE IN ITS VEINS
Many Antarctic fish have "antifreeze" molecules in their bodies that enable them to live in a "super-cooled" state; their body fluids remain liquid at temperatures below the point at which ice forms. Antarctic ice fish (such as the fish on the left) have almost translucent (see-through) blood.

Hair under paws keeps fox from sinking in snow; the fox's Latin name is Alopex lagopus. Lagopus means "hairy foot"

Sharp claws to dig through the snow to find food

A BIRD FOR ALL SEASONS
A ptarmigan's plumage changes twice a year so that it is well camouflaged at all times. Also, the density of its feathers increases in the winter. When resting overnight, ptarmigans sometimes burrow in snow to reduce heat loss.

Rock ptarmigan
Lagopus mutus

Dense fur coat with long hairs traps body warmth

Ears are furry inside and out for extra warmth

FINE TO BE FAT
Whales and seals are kept warm by a layer of thick fat called blubber. This fat walrus is in no danger of getting cold. Walruses can weigh up to 1.8 tons (1,600 kg), with tusks 3 ft (1 m) long.

Small, round ears and a short muzzle cut down on heat loss; foxes from warmer places have larger ears and a longer muzzle

Sharp, pointed teeth to grab animals such as lemmings

DOUBLE-GLAZED FUR
The Arctic fox's white winter fur is made up of hairs that are hollow inside, full of air. The air in the hairs traps body warmth from the fox in much the same way as a double-glazed window traps warmth from houses. Air is a good insulator and does not let heat escape easily. The Arctic fox can tolerate temperatures of -40°F (-40°C), or even lower, quite comfortably.

17

Survival of the fittest

Pale maidens
Sisyrinchium filifolium

Flowers are
both male
and female

Capsules
contain seeds

ONLY SPECIALIZED, HARDY PLANTS can
survive the fierce winds, biting cold, thin soils,
and short growing season of the polar lands.
The most successful plants are the simple ones,
such as mosses, lichens, and algae. Arctic and
Antarctic plants often grow in low, compact cushions,
called tussocks, which keep out of the freezing, drying
winds, trap available moisture, and resist being
crushed by snow and ice. In the short summer, flowers
burst open and rapidly produce seeds before the
winter weather returns. Few pollinating insects live in
these cold places, so many plants reproduce from small
pieces of themselves, such as runners or bulbils. The
wind may also spread their pollen.

Plant grows
low to the
ground to
stay out of
the wind

Long roots
obtain
nitrogen
and water
in dry,
harsh
conditions

Root system
anchors plant
firmly in soil

Arctic wormwood
Artemisia borealis

PALE MAIDENS
This sub-
Antarctic plant of
the iris family
has grasslike
leaves. It is
able to store
food in
fleshy roots
underground.
This ability
helps it
survive the
cold and dry
seasons and
grow quickly
in the spring.

Flower heads are
about 0.25 in (5
to 6 mm) across

SEEDS AWAY
The northern primrose,
Primula scandanavica,
produces many seeds in a
capsule. When ripe, the
capsule splits open and
releases the seeds.

FAST FLOWERS
Calandria feltonii
is native to the
Falkland Islands north of
Antarctica, which have a
cool temperate climate. A
succession of short-lived
flowers open quickly
when the sun shines.

Fleshy
leaves
store
water

Silky or hairless
leaves are
deeply divided

ARCTIC WORMWOOD
This hardy plant, which grows
throughout the Northern
Hemisphere, is sometimes
known as Arctic wormwood.
It grows in colonies on dry,
rocky ridges and gravel banks.

Woolly bear
caterpillar
Arctia caja

PLANT EATER
Several species of butterflies
and moths live in the
Arctic regions.

*Branched
flower head
is called a
panicle*

Northern fleabane
Erigeron borealis

*Side branches
have spikelets
on stalks*

*Daisylike
flowers made
up of small
flowers
called florets*

GROWTH OF GRASS
The most successful
plants in the cold polar
regions are the low-
lying mosses and
lichens. However,
several grasses, such
as *Deschampsia
cespitosa*, thrive in
the Arctic. On the
Antarctic mainland
only one grass
survives, *Deschampsia
flexuosa*, or Antarctic
wavy-hair grass.

Slipperwort
Calceolaria fothergillii

*Flower sticks
out from leaves
so insects can
spot the flower
easily*

*Large lower
petals look
like a slipper*

INSECT REPELLENT
Low cushions of northern fleabane bloom in
the Arctic summer, when the tundra becomes
waterlogged and water collects on its surface.
The plant is highly unattractive to fleas and
midges, hence its name, and it is used
successfully by humans as an insect repellent.

*Hairy leaves
trap warmth
and moisture*

SLIPPERWORT
The rare and beautiful slipperwort grows
along the coasts of the Falkland Islands.
The color of the large, slipperlike lower
petal attracts insects, which helps the plant
reproduce. When an insect feeds on the
plant's nectar, pollen sticks to its legs and
is carried to another slipper flower.

TREELESS TUNDRA
The tundra is a broad zone of low-growing
vegetation lying immediately south of the Arctic
Ocean across northern Eurasia and North
America, where the harsh climate, severe
winds, and shallow, frozen soils prevent trees
from growing. The small plants of the tundra
grow slowly and are nearly all perennial
(live longer than a year).

Birds of the Arctic

FEW BIRDS CAN SURVIVE the hostile Arctic climate all year round, but residents include the ptarmigan, raven, ivory gull, and dovekie. The plumage of Arctic residents is more dense than that of migratory species, especially in the winter. Their feet are protected by feathers and do not freeze to the ice. Most Arctic birds, such as shorebirds, ducks, geese, swans, and gulls, are migratory. Some migrants, particularly waders, travel long journeys in the winter, as far as South America, South Africa, and Australasia. In the summer, Arctic birds take advantage of the rich insect and small-mammal life on the tundra, nesting and rapidly rearing young before the winter sets in. Many different types of bird can feed and nest in close proximity because they share the available food—for instance, geese eat plants, seabirds eat fish, and waders eat invertebrates.

LIKE A BIRD
In 1926, the airship *Norge* carried Norwegian Roald Amundsen and Italian Umberto Nobile over the North Pole.

HAPPY FAMILIES
The dovekie (*Alle alle*) is not much bigger than a thrush, but there are a lot of them! Over 100 million dovekies, or little auks, breed along Arctic coasts each summer. In the winter, they move south but usually stay near the Arctic Circle. Dovekies have a thick layer of fat under their skin to keep them warm. They feed on small invertebrates and fish, storing food in a throat pouch.

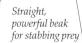

Straight, powerful beak for stabbing prey

Long neck to probe in water beds

ON DISPLAY
Cranes mate for life. They perform spectacular courtship dances—head bobbing, bowing, skipping, and sometimes leaping as high as 20 ft (6 m) in the air.

REDHEADS
Sandhill cranes (*Grus canadensis*) breed mostly in the remote Arctic, laying their eggs in mounds of grass or other plants in an undisturbed marsh. Young birds stay with their parents for nearly a year. The sandhill crane's plumage often appears rusty because of reddish iron oxide stains from the water of tundra ponds. The birds probe with their bills in the mud for worms, water creatures, and frogs, then transfer the stain to their feathers when preening.

Streamlined, torpedo-shaped body allows fast underwater swimming

A BIRD IN THE NET
Arctic birds were an invaluable source of food for Inuit people. Hunters often caught the birds in nets on long poles.

Moving the two sticks back and forth causes the birds to bob down for their food

TOY TIME
Carving is an ancient Inuit art that often shows Arctic birds and mammals. The villages of Holman Island and Cape Dorset in Canada have become well known for their style of art. To make this bird-feeding toy work, the two sticks are moved back and forth.

Powerful, slender, dagger-shaped beak snaps up fish and crustaceans

FEATHER BEDS
Eider ducks (*Somateria mollissima*) in the Arctic are migratory, whereas in warmer places they stay near their breeding grounds all year. Eider ducks feed mainly on shellfish, which they swallow whole. Muscles in the bird's stomach crush the shellfish. Eider ducks have particularly soft and dense down feathers for warmth. Female eiders pluck some of their breast feathers to line their nests. People use these feathers to fill quilts.

LOONY BIRDS
Loons, such as this black-throated Arctic loon, are sometimes called divers. Loons are adapted to swimming underwater after their prey but are clumsy on land because their legs are set so far back on the body. The name loon may come from the Icelandic word *lomr*, meaning lame or clumsy. The Arctic loon breeds on tundra lakes and migrates mainly to the Pacific coast in the winter.

Handsome breeding plumage; winter plumage is dull and grayish

WATER LOVERS
Loons spend most of their lives on the water and come on land only to nest. Puffins (foreground) are also excellent swimmers and divers, hunting for small shoaling fish such as sand eels. They are ungainly on land but are able to jump from rock to rock.

Birds of the Antarctic

THE MOST COMMON ANTARCTIC BIRDS are seabirds, such as penguins, albatrosses, and petrels, which come ashore in the summer to breed in remote, predator-free locations. They take advantage of the seas around Antarctica, which are packed with food for hungry chicks. Only 13 species of flying bird make use of ice-free land for nesting on the Antarctic mainland. The rest squash into colonies on cramped sub-Antarctic islands. Antarctic birds rely on their dense feathers and frostbite-resistant feet to stay warm, while fat reserves in the skin act as both food and insulation. Most Antarctic birds leave during the cold winter months. But some, including emperor penguins, king penguins, and wandering albatrosses, stay behind to complete their long breeding cycle. Others, such as sheathbills, only just manage to survive in the freezing winter conditions.

ANTARCTIC SCAVENGERS
Giant petrels are nicknamed "stinkers" because of their unpleasant smell. They use their powerful hooked beaks for feeding and scavenging, as well as for killing other birds. Petrels will eat almost anything, including dead seals and whales. A petrel is about the size of a vulture, with a wingspan of nearly 6.5 ft (2 m).

Wings are held up like a Viking helmet, making the bird appear large and fierce

Earsplitting shriek warns enemies to stay away

Powerful hooked beak stabs and kills prey

Antarctic skua
Catharacta maccormicki

Wings are spread to display white patches

PIRATES OF THE SKIES
Peculiar doglike barking calls signal the arrival of a pair of skuas. Skuas earn their reputation as "pirates of the skies" by chasing other birds and forcing them to regurgitate (bring up) their food. These large, aggressive birds are also notorious for stealing the eggs and young of other birds. Two skuas may even cooperate while hunting, using clever tricks to snatch a meal more easily.

Brown skua
Catharacta lonnbergi

NOT FUSSY
Sheathbills are the only land birds
that live year-round in Antarctica.
Their success is due to their varied
diet, which includes penguin and
seal feces, penguin eggs, chicks,
dead fish, krill, and limpets.
Sheathbills also steal food
intended for penguin chicks.

*Horny sheath
protects nostrils*

*Orange growths at base
of beak become brighter
during breeding season*

*Jagged, hooked
bill helps grip
slippery fish*

Blue-eyed cormorant
Phalacrocorax atriceps

*Wings are spread out
to dry off after a swim*

*Feathers soak up water
and allow the cormorant
to dive more easily*

Tern

Albatross

Shearwater

Cormorant

Penguin

DIFFERENT STROKES
The pursuit of a fishy meal involves a different
technique for every type of bird. Cormorants use
their strong feet to paddle deep underwater after
prey; penguins dive deep, then propel themselves
through the sea using their wings. A tern picks fish by
plunging down just under the surface of the water, and
albatrosses float on the surface, keeping a sharp eye
out for any possible food. Shearwaters spot their
prey from the air and then plunge in pursuit.

SEAWEED NEST
Blue-eyed cormorants nest in smelly, noisy colonies close
to the sea, building untidy nests of seaweed, lichens,
mosses, and feathers glued together with guano (bird
excrement). Blue-eyed cormorants breed on the Antarctic
Peninsula and on a number of Antarctic and sub-Antarctic
islands. Some use their nesting sites
all year round, roosting there
throughout the winter. This
allows them to stay near
their fishing grounds
in open water.

Snowy owl
Bubo scandiacus

Lords of the skies

THE HUGE SUMMER BREEDING COLONIES of birds in both the Arctic and the Antarctic attract a number of predatory birds quick to enjoy the easy meals of eggs and chicks. In the Arctic, the small mammals of the tundra lands, such as lemmings and hares, increase the range of food for birds to hunt. The variety of predatory birds is therefore greater in the Arctic than in the Antarctic and includes eagles, skuas, owls, falcons, and buzzards. The predators time their own breeding cycle to coincide with that of their prey, to ensure that their chicks will always have plenty to eat.

GHOSTLY HUNTER
Snowy owls feed primarily on the millions of lemmings living on the Arctic tundra. Owl population usually follows the rise and fall of the lemming population on its three- to four-year cycle (p. 36). Many of these owls wander far south in the winter.

Soapstone and ivory owl carved by Inuit craftsman in Cape Dorset, Canada

Feathers at tips of wings spread out like fingers to help the eagle push and steer through the air

Spread feathers help the bird reduce speed

Lethal curved talons grip, crush, and carry off prey

Broad wings give both speed and control in flight

Strong legs cushion impact of landing

The golden eagle slows in midair and spreads out its wings and tail to act as a brake

Eyes focused firmly on its destination, the eagle further brakes its flight by swinging out its lower body and legs

At the last moment, its feet swing down to grip the perch

WATCH OUT BELOW
Golden eagles fly at low altitudes while hunting, then swoop suddenly to pounce on their prey. This swoop-and-grab attack is effective because it happens so swiftly that the prey is often taken by surprise. Here, a golden eagle is landing on a branch in much the same way as it would when diving for a meal.

KING OF THE CLOUDS
As the most powerful and majestic bird in the sky, the eagle features in countless stories, myths, and legends. In this illustration by British artist Reginald Knowles, a magnificent eagle perches in a tree. It appears on the title page of a collection of Norse legends.

Golden eagle
Aquila chrysaetos

Sharp eyes spot birds and animals moving on the ground below

Hooked bill can tear flesh from prey

Huge chest muscles drive the enormous wings

Gyrfalcon
Falco rusticolus

Feathers down to toes keep the feet warm

BIGGEST AND BEST
Gyrfalcon, the most powerful of the falcons, relies on power and speed to catch its victims. It usually kills its prey in flight.

A KILLING MACHINE
A magnificent flier, the golden eagle is a fierce predator of ptarmigan and other birds, as well as small mammals, such as ground squirrels and hares. The golden eagle ranges widely across the Northern Hemisphere, living in forests and grasslands as well as tundra. It is usually tree-nesting, but in tundra regions, it nests directly on the ground.

FALCON FOOD
The rock ptarmigan (*Lagopus mutus*) is the gyrfalcon's main prey.

Ocean wanderer

THE HUGE, GENTLE ALBATROSSES of the Antarctic seas come ashore only to breed. They do not breed on the Antarctic landmass itself but on islands such as South Georgia, just north of the pack ice. There are six species of albatross that breed in the Antarctic: the black-browed, gray-headed, yellow-nosed, wandering, sooty, and light-mantled sooty. Probably about 750,000 pairs of birds breed each year. The main advantage of these isolated locations is safety from predators. Albatrosses raise only one chick at a time. The chick takes a long time to mature, sometimes remaining in the nest for up to a year. Chicks are protected from the intense cold by thick down feathers and an insulating layer of blubber, or fat. When winter begins, most albatrosses set off over the southern oceans once more.

DEAD WEIGHT
Sailors believed albatrosses brought them good luck. In Coleridge's *The Rime of the Ancient Mariner,* the unlucky mariner is forced to wear an albatross he has killed.

Black-browed albatross
Diomedea melanophris

Webbed feet held wide to push against the air and act as brakes

BUMPY LANDING
Landing is a difficult task for a bird so well adapted to flying over the sea. When albatrosses approach the nest site, they circle around several times before putting their legs down, like the landing gear on an aircraft. But they often land with a bump.

Gray-headed albatross
Thalassarche chrysostoma

Large eyes indicate sharp eyesight necessary for spotting food in the sea

BIRD MAN
People have always wanted to fly like birds, but this design for an early flying machine was no challenge to the albatross's mastery of the air. For birds, like airplanes, takeoff and landing are the most dangerous parts of flying. Because of their enormous wingspan and body weight, albatrosses also need a runway to gather enough speed for takeoff.

Tube-shaped nostrils have glands at the base that excrete excess salt

Bill has razor-sharp edges and catches fish and squid

LIVING THE HIGH LIFE
Although gray-headed albatrosses weigh only half as much as wandering albatrosses, they still find it hard to take off, so they live on steep cliff sides and get extra lift from the strong winds rising up over the cliffs. Because of the harsh conditions, only half their chicks survive, a rate that is not unusually low for Antarctic birds.

During courtship, the bird points its beak to the sky and moos like a cow

FAITHFUL FLYING ACE

The wandering albatross has the greatest wingspan of any living bird. Its wing power enables the bird to cover over 300 miles (500 km) a day, alighting on the sea to feed in calm weather. Like all albatrosses, it comes ashore only to breed. The breeding cycle is exceptionally long, taking a year to complete. It therefore breeds only every 2 years. Breeding is preceded by an elaborate courtship display, in which the two birds dance face to face, making a variety of sounds and clapping their beaks together loudly. Wandering albatrosses usually pair for life. The most elaborate displays take place among newly formed pairs; old established partners are more discreet.

Wingspan may be between 8 ft 4 in and 11 ft 10 in (254 to 360 cm)

SECONDHAND FOOD

Parent albatrosses feed their young by regurgitating (bringing up) the food they eat, in the form of a sticky, oily mixture. This feeding takes place when they return to the nest after many hours, or even days, of fishing out at sea. Both adults and young can use this smelly and sticky oil for defense, ejecting it with reasonable accuracy over a 6-ft (2-m) range. Predators, such as skuas, may be repelled by the foul smell or immobilized if the sticky oil saturates their feathers.

Mother feeds regurgitated krill to chick

Nest is lined with grass and feathers

Nest is about 12 in (30 cm) high

BARREL NEST

The black-browed albatross makes a raised nest of mud and straw among the tussock grass.

Wandering albatross
Diomedea exulans

Strong legs and wide feet assist landing and swimming

Penguin parade

ONE OF THE MOST SPECTACULAR SIGHTS of the Antarctic is the millions of penguins gathered at their noisy summer breeding colonies. Only two species, the Adélie and the emperor, breed on the Antarctic continent itself, but the gentoo, macaroni, chinstrap, rockhopper, and king penguins all breed within Antarctic waters. Emperor and king penguins lay a single egg each year; the other species usually lay two eggs. Penguins are amazingly well adapted for swimming in cold seas. Some of their adaptations, especially the dense, waterproof feathers and thick fat layers under the skin, also serve them well on land. The penguins rely on the fat as an energy supply when they are caring for eggs and chicks and cannot get out to sea to obtain food for themselves.

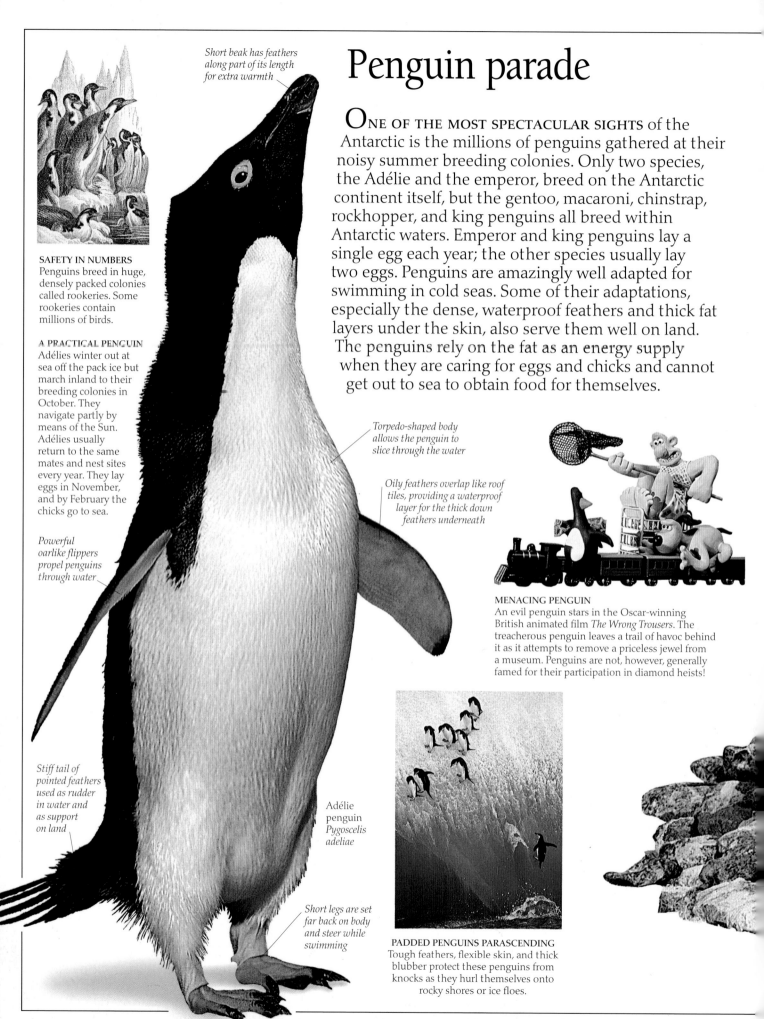

Short beak has feathers along part of its length for extra warmth

SAFETY IN NUMBERS
Penguins breed in huge, densely packed colonies called rookeries. Some rookeries contain millions of birds.

A PRACTICAL PENGUIN
Adélies winter out at sea off the pack ice but march inland to their breeding colonies in October. They navigate partly by means of the Sun. Adélies usually return to the same mates and nest sites every year. They lay eggs in November, and by February the chicks go to sea.

Powerful oarlike flippers propel penguins through water

Torpedo-shaped body allows the penguin to slice through the water

Oily feathers overlap like roof tiles, providing a waterproof layer for the thick down feathers underneath

Stiff tail of pointed feathers used as rudder in water and as support on land

Adélie penguin
Pygoscelis adeliae

Short legs are set far back on body and steer while swimming

MENACING PENGUIN
An evil penguin stars in the Oscar-winning British animated film *The Wrong Trousers*. The treacherous penguin leaves a trail of havoc behind it as it attempts to remove a priceless jewel from a museum. Penguins are not, however, generally famed for their participation in diamond heists!

PADDED PENGUINS PARASCENDING
Tough feathers, flexible skin, and thick blubber protect these penguins from knocks as they hurl themselves onto rocky shores or ice floes.

King penguin
*Aptenodytes
patagonica*

Gentoo penguin
Pygoscelis papua

Rockhopper penguin
Eudyptes chrysocome

MARK OF DISTINCTION
The main distinguishing
marks of penguins are
on the head and upper
breast, so the birds are
identifiable when they
swim on the surface.
They use their colors
and head crests for
species recognition and
for courtship displays.

KING PENGUINS
Kings have golden-orange
patches on their ears and
bill. The long bill is useful for
catching speedy fish and squid.

GENTOO PENGUINS
The pink bill of gentoos is
dagger-shaped to catch fish and
krill. Gentoos can swim at speeds
of up to 16 mph (27 kph).

ROCKHOPPER PENGUINS
Rockhoppers have conspicuous
yellow eyebrows that they use
for courtship display. They are
the smallest polar penguin.

PREDATION
Adult penguins need to
defend their eggs and chicks
from predators such as skuas
(right). In the oceans,
penguins are prey to
leopard seals, sea lions,
and killer whales.

NOISY NESTERS
Chinstrap penguins are good
climbers, using their beaks and
sharp claws to reach nest sites
in high rocky places. They are
noisy and aggressive penguins.
They often take over the
nesting sites of Adélies or
steal stones from one
another's nests.

*Black feathers
form a
"chinstrap"
across
white
breast*

*Shallow
nest lined
with
stones and
vegetation*

Chinstrap
penguin
*Pygoscelis
antarctica*

Emperors of the Antarctic

IN EARLY APRIL, when most of Antarctica's wildlife heads north, the emperor penguin begins its 60-mile (100-km) trek south to its traditional nesting sites on the sea ice. To reach the breeding colony, the birds must cover a huge area of sea ice in pitch darkness. In early May, the female lays her eggs and returns north to the open sea. The male then undertakes an incredible feat of endurance. During the icy winter, he incubates the egg on his feet under a flap of warm skin. This means that for 2 months, the male cannot feed and may lose up to half his body weight. The female returns to feed the hatched chick in July. Each pair of emperors rears one chick a year, but only about one out of five survives.

FEET HEAT
Chicks stand on the adults' feet until they are about 8 weeks old, hiding under a brood pouch, or flap of skin, for extra warmth and protection. Older chicks rely on their dense, fluffy feathers and the warm bodies of fellow chicks to keep them warm, while their parents search for food.

TRULY MAJESTIC
The emperor, the largest penguin, stands nearly 4 ft (1.2 m) tall and weighs 65 lb (30 kg). It can spend up to 18 minutes underwater and dive to over 850 ft (260 m).

Birds in the center are the warmest of the group

A tightly packed group can reduce heat loss by as much as 50 percent

Any bird that fails to join the huddle during the winter months faces certain death

Birds take turns occupying the most exposed position

Emperors tend to turn their backs on the constantly shifting wind

TOGETHERNESS
Incubating males huddle together for warmth, moving very little in order to conserve energy. When the chicks are born, the birds still huddle together as much as possible. Some emperor colonies contain over 20,000 pairs.

After the females return, the skinny and hungry males make their way to the open sea

Penguin "flies" out of the water to draw breath

Penguin catches fish and krill in its beak

Underwater, penguin steers with its feet and tail

Penguin shoots onto land or ice in giant leap of up to 7 ft (2 m)

DUCKING AND DIVING
Penguins "fly" through the water, propelled by their stiff flippers. When swimming fast, they often use a technique called porpoising, leaping out of the water like dolphins or porpoises. Air offers less resistance to movement than water, so porpoising penguins can travel at speeds of 18 mph (30 kph).

Bill is small to cut
down on heat loss

Emperor penguin
Aptenodytes forsteri

*In the
nasal cavities,
much of the
warm air that
would otherwise
be lost in
breathing is
recycled*

*Closely packed,
overlapping
feathers cover a
thick layer of
blubber*

Feet are small
to cut down on
heat loss

King of the Arctic

The polar bear is one of the largest and most powerful hunters of the Arctic lands; an average male weighs as much as six adult people. Polar bears are found across the Arctic region, and some even roam as far as the North Pole. They are solitary animals except in the breeding season. They do not hibernate, and in the long winter, when the sea is at its greatest extent, they hunt for seals coming up for air at breathing holes in the ice. Their dense fur keeps them warm even in the most severe conditions. An undercoat of thick fur is protected by an outer coat of long guard hairs. These hairs stick together when they get wet, forming a waterproof barrier. Under the fur, a thick layer of blubber performs two roles—insulating the bear against the cold and acting as a food store to help the bear survive hard times.

The small, rounded ears lose little body heat

Mature female polar bear
Thalarctos maritimus

HEAVYWEIGHT
An average adult male polar bear measures 8 ft (2.5 m) from head to tail and weighs over 1,000 lb (about 500 kg). The largest males grow up to 10 ft (3 m) in length and can weigh up to 2,000 lb (900 kg). Female polar bears are much smaller than the males.

Female keeps floor clean by covering it with freshly scraped snow

Air vent scraped in roof lets stale air escape

Female first digs the tunnel, then hollows out the chamber

Pointed teeth capable of killing prey

BEARING ARMS
By playing, cubs gain strength and practice skills they will need when they are adults. Young bears often wrestle in the snow with their mouths wide open to show off their sharp teeth. Such fights rarely result in injury. Finding and killing prey is not easy, and bears have developed a bad reputation for raiding human settlements in search of food.

CAVE CUBS
Polar bear cubs are born in December or January in a warm, cozy den dug in the snow by the mother. The cubs grow rapidly on their mother's rich milk, which is about 30 percent fat. While in the ice cave, the mother has nothing to eat and lives on the stored fat in her body.

CAPABLE CLIMBER
In spite of their huge size, polar bears are able to climb trees, such as this one at Cape Churchill on Hudson Bay in Canada. Between 600 and 1,000 bears gather here in October to wait for the bay to freeze over so that they can head out over the ice to hunt.

Thick fur prevents bear from being scratched

Back legs are especially strong

POLAR PADDLE
Polar bears are slow but very strong swimmers, able to keep swimming for a long time. The bears use only their front legs to propel themselves; the back legs are held still like a rudder.

SEAL SLAYER
Polar bears are clever and patient hunters. Over 90 percent of their diet consists of seals. They wait by a seal's blowhole in the ice, pouncing as soon as it comes up for air. One stroke of the bear's massive paw and a bite at the back of the skull kill the seal. But most hunting trips are unsuccessful, and a bear may not eat for 5 days.

White fur turns a little yellow in captive animals, such as this one

Hollow hairs trap warm air near body

Thickly padded soles covered by rough skin and sometimes tough hair

Sharp claws

Nonslip soles help grip slippery ice

The mighty moose

Flat shape gives moose a stable surface with which to push rivals

The bell is a fold of skin covered with hair

THE MOOSE IS THE LARGEST MEMBER of the deer family. It stands up to 7.5 ft (2.4 m) tall and can weigh up to 1,800 lb (825 kg). The moose can be found throughout the northern United States and Canada, and in northern Europe and Asia, where it is sometimes called elk. In Europe and Asia, the moose lives mainly in the coniferous forests bordering the tundra. In North America, some populations range widely over the tundra, spending long periods on the shores of the Arctic Ocean in midsummer, when flies are likely to plague it farther inland. When winters are especially harsh, moose often move farther south in search of food, to areas that have lighter snow cover. Moose are solitary animals, and their population density is low. Because of their immense size, they need a relatively large area to themselves to enable them to find an adequate food supply. However, in the winter, when in search of new food supplies, they will often travel in a group, covering considerable distances.

LETHAL WEAPONS
The bull moose has heavy, flat antlers. It uses them more for fighting rival males during the breeding season than for protection. The moose sheds its antlers every year and grows a new set. By late August, the antlers are fully grown, and the bull strips off the "velvet" covering and polishes his great weapons against a tree.

Undersurface of moose's foot

SURE-FOOTED
The moose has long and sharply pointed hooves, in contrast to those of its relative—the reindeer—which are rounded. The pointed hooves help the moose grip ice and snow.

Moose
Alces alces

Calf remains close to mother for several months

Reddish-brown coat becomes darker as the calf matures

Long legs allow even young moose to walk easily through deep snow

MAKING MORE MOOSE
The mating season of the moose lasts for 4–8 weeks in the fall. The bull wanders around looking for and calling to females (cows); the cows return the calls. The bull will follow every sound to see if it was made by a cow or a rival bull. Baby moose are born in late May and June. The mother carries the baby for about 7½ months before the birth. There is usually one calf, although twins and even triplets are not uncommon. When the calf is about 10 days old, it can travel with its mother.

Antlers appear only in males and can spread to as much as 6 ft 8 in (2.05 m)

Antlers are not fully grown and are still heavily covered with velvet

MONEY MOOSE
The moose is such a revered animal in many northern European countries that it has even been featured on banknotes. This note comes from Lithuania.

Muzzle hangs 3 to 4 in (8 to 10 cm) over its chin

Short neck, coupled with long legs, means that moose has to get on its knees to eat low-growing plants

SOLITARY GIANT
Within the tundra, the preferred habitat of moose is land that contains willow swamps and lakes. Moose are good swimmers and can cross lakes and rivers with ease. They like to roll in mud holes, which helps them get rid of any small parasitic animals. In the summer, they eat leaves and tender twigs, as well as grass and herbs. Because of their great size and dangerous antlers, they have few natural predators, with the exception of humans. Wolves may occasionally attack isolated moose and the young, although the antlers of the male make it a formidable foe.

Arctic willow
Salix arctica

FAVORITE FOOD
Arctic willow (*Salix arctica*) and Alaska willow (*Salix alaxensis*) are the favorite foods of the moose.

Moose is beginning to lose the velvet on its antlers

WATER WADERS
Moose are often to be found standing up to their knees in water. This helps them get rid of the flies that trouble them greatly in the warm summer months, but they also feed on the aquatic vegetation. An adult will consume up to 43 lb (19.5 kg) of vegetation a day. Sometimes, they retreat into water to escape from predators such as wolves.

Tundra mammals

Limit of permanent ice
Limit of drift ice
Timberline
Tundra

Arctic Circle

Canada

Arctic Ocean

Greenland

Russia

THE ONLY LAND MAMMAL that can live out on the Arctic sea ice is the polar bear. However, several mammals live on the Arctic tundra (pp. 8–9), both as residents and migrants. During the summer in the Arctic, a great deal of the ice on the tundra melts, plants begin to grow, and insect eggs hatch. This means that suddenly there is plenty of food for animals that have spent all winter on the tundra, as well as for the migrants who arrive as soon as the snows melt. For much of the summer, the Sun never sets (pp. 6–7), therefore animals can feed around the clock. It is necessary for them to do this so that the young can grow as quickly as possible, because the summer is short and the land soon freezes over again.

TUNDRA VEGETATION
The tundra consists of a nearly continuous, though at times thin, cover of vegetation. Sedges, such as the Arctic cottongrass (*Eriophorum angustifolium*) predominate, together with true grasses. Scattered among the grasses are various mosses, a variety of flowering herbs, and a few species of dwarf shrubs and willows.

SEA OF ICE
The central area of the Arctic Ocean remains permanently frozen. The tundra, which spans North America and Eurasia, is covered in snow and ice in the winter but is green in the summer. No trees grow on the tundra because it is too cold and windy, even in the summer months.

Long, pointed ears enable the lynx to hear well in dense, muffling snow

FELINE VISITOR
The Canadian lynx (*Lynx canadensis*) is mainly a creature of the forest that borders areas of the tundra in North America, but it is often found in the true tundra during the summer months. Its brown coat blends in well with the tundra landscape in the summer, and in the winter the coat becomes thicker and lighter so that the lynx is hard to see against the snow.

In the winter big feet are covered with thick fur that acts like a snowshoe

Snowshoe hare
Lepus americanus

HARE LINE
Three types of hare inhabit the tundra—the snowshoe hare, the rare Alaskan hare, and the common Arctic hare. Hares grow white winter coats and have well-developed claws that enable them to dig through the snow for food.

Lemmings are very common on the tundra

ACCIDENTAL DEATH
Every few years, driven by population pressures and food shortages, large numbers of lemmings try to migrate to new areas. Many drown while attempting to swim across broad rivers, but despite the popular belief, they are not trying to commit suicide.

TURNCOAT
The stoat (*Mustela erminea*) is protected from harsh weather in its home beneath the snow. It is often called "ermine" when its coat is in its white winter phase. It is a cute-looking animal, but a ruthless hunter. The stoat's slimness enables it to pursue lemmings, its main prey in the Arctic, through the lemmings' networks of underground tunnels.

GREAT BEAR
The word "Arctic" comes from the Greek word *Arctikos*, meaning "pertaining to the constellation of the bear." The extensive star constellation Ursa Major, the Great Bear, is visible only in the Northern Hemisphere.

GLUTTON OF THE ARCTIC
The wolverine (*Gulo gulo*), a distant relative of the stoat, looks like a small bear. Wolverines are solitary animals and usually meet others only to mate during the summer. They are relentless hunters, able to pursue their victims for many miles without tiring. Their main prey is reindeer. After a kill, wolverines eat much of the flesh on the spot, but they hide the remainder for another day, earning themselves a reputation for gluttony. Wolverine fur is highly prized.

Sometimes the fur is tipped silvery white

Bears have sensitive noses and a strong sense of smell

Powerful jaws and teeth allow bear to eat a variety of foods

SLEEPYHEAD
The brown, or grizzly, bear (*Ursus arctos*) has a wide geographical range, including the tundra regions of Alaska, Canada, and parts of Russia. They eat a wide variety of small mammals, fish, insects, and plants, depending on the season and the area in which they live. In the winter months, the grizzly digs a snug den in the ground and hibernates, taking approximately 2 weeks to enter a deep winter sleep. During hibernation, the body temperature drops and the bear lives off its reserves of stored fat. It sometimes sleeps for as long as 7 months.

Long claws on the front paws help the bear to dig

Bears often stand upright on the soles of their back feet

Reindeer and caribou

REINDEER ARE CALLED CARIBOU in North America. The name "caribou" may come from *xalibu*, the Native American Micmac word for "the animal that paws through snow for its food." Wild reindeer still survive on the frozen tundra of North America, Siberia, and Scandinavia, but they have also been domesticated in Scandinavia and Siberia for thousands of years. Although their thick coats insulate them against the Arctic cold, many populations migrate south in the winter to find food and shelter. As they travel, their coats grow thick and gray. In the summer, reindeer are plagued by hordes of insects, such as mosquitoes and warble flies, as they graze on the tundra meadows. Their main predator is the wolf. Reindeer are the only deer in which both sexes grow antlers.

REINDEER STAR
The most famous reindeer in the world is probably red-nosed Rudolph, the reindeer who leads Santa Claus's sleigh.

Antler buds appear two weeks after the old ones are shed

New antlers are covered by soft, thick velvet

Fully formed antlers are bone-hard

TITLE FIGHT
In the fall rutting, or mating, season, bulls, with their antlers locked together, wrestle to decide which is the strongest. The winner of these contests collects a group of cows for mating and then defends his harem from all challengers.

BIG, BIGGER, BIGGEST
Antlers are shed each year. Bulls shed their antlers at the end of the year, but the cows wait until spring. New antlers grow rapidly and are fully grown by the start of the fall rutting season.

Nuclear explosion

NUCLEAR POLLUTION
In 1986, a nuclear reactor at Chernobyl in Ukraine exploded. Lichens and mosses absorbed radioactive Cesium 137. Reindeer ate the lichens, which made them sick and their meat unfit to eat.

Reindeer moss (*Cladonia* species) absorbed radioactivity from the air

Velvet contains blood vessels to nourish the growing antlers

Reindeer, or caribou
Rangifer tarandus

LICHEN LUNCH
Reindeer feed largely on lichens, which are one of the few foods available throughout the Arctic winter. Some reindeer living on Arctic islands will also eat seaweed. In the summer, a wider variety of plants are available. Adult reindeer eat about 10 lb (4.5 kg) of food a day to get the energy they need.

Sensitive nose helps reindeer find food, even under the snow

CEREMONIAL APRON
This shaman's ceremonial apron was made from reindeer hide. The shaman was a powerful figure in the culture of many native Siberian and North American peoples. It was believed that he could get power from supernatural beings that were everywhere on land, and even lurked beneath the sea.

Iron symbols of the sun, fish, and diving birds decorate apron

Heat is lost rapidly through antlers in velvet, cooling the reindeer on hot summer days

Hollow hairs contain air that traps body heat

SWIMMING CHAMPIONS
Migrating reindeer have to cross many fast-flowing rivers. They are strong swimmers, plunging into the icy waters without any hesitation. The reindeers' broad feet help them swim against the current, and the hollow hairs in their coats help them float more easily.

Iron-bladed reindeer skin scraper used by Siberian Tungus tribe

Lapp stick with spadelike blade to probe under the snow for food

TOOLS OF THE TRADE
Many Scandinavian and Siberian peoples relied on reindeer for food, clothing, and shelter. They devised many tools specifically to enable them take full advantage of their domesticated animals.

Muzzle covered with fine, warm hair

Dense, waterproof coat turns grayish-white in winter

Sharp hooves grip ice and dig through snow for food

GROWING UP FAST
Calves are born in June and grow fast on their mothers' rich milk, which is four times as nutritious as cow's milk. Calves can keep up with the movements of the herd when they are 1–2 days old and are better protected from predators such as wolves if they remain within the herd's safety. Calves stay with their mothers for about a year, growing their first antlers when they are around 2 months old.

Broad feet fringed with fur keep reindeer from sinking into snow

Company of wolves

BLENDING INTO THE BACKGROUND
In the Arctic areas of North America and Eurasia, wolves often have white coats for camouflage. Because the animals they hunt cannot see them easily, the wolves can get very close to their prey. In the forests to the south of the tundra, the wolves have gray or even blackish fur.

Wolves are intelligent, adaptable animals with a wide natural range. Arctic populations rely on their thick fur and cooperative hunting techniques to survive. They generally live in packs of between 8 and 20 family members. They are bonded together by affection for each other, and by a ranking system of near-military precision. Pack members establish their rank at almost every meeting: a dominant or high-ranking wolf stands erect, ears and tail pointing upward, and may show its teeth, then growl. A subordinate or low-ranking wolf crouches, holds its tail between its legs, and turns down its ears; instead of growling, it whines. A wolf pack ranges over a specific area, picking off sick, aged, or injured herd animals. Needlessly feared and persecuted by humans for thousands of years, wolves kill only to survive and do not deserve their bad reputation—they are, in fact, the ancestors of all domesticated dogs.

RING OF HORN
Wolves are expert hunters and prey chiefly on large hooved animals such as caribou, moose, and muskoxen. To defend themselves from a wolf pack, a herd of muskoxen forms a tight circle, with the wolves on the outside and the females and young in the center. By panicking the muskoxen, the wolves can break the circle and reach the calves inside. But if a wolf is caught by one of the muskoxen's horns, it can be tossed into the air and then trampled.

Mouth remains wide open during howling

Wolf
Canis lupus

Wolf throws back its head in order to howl

IN HARMONY
An eerie howl in the night echoes through countless horror films, striking terror into the hearts of the audience. In fact, howling is simply one of the ways in which wolves communicate with one another. Wolf speak ranges from whimpers and growls to complex facial and body expressions. Wolves howl in order to keep in touch with pack members or to warn other packs to keep out of the area. If one wolf howls, the others join in, often harmonizing with each other. The variety of sound makes the pack seem bigger and more formidable.

LEADER OF THE PACK
The wolf's instinct for power and freedom has inspired countless writers. The American novelist Jack London (1876–1916) wrote his novel *The Call of the Wild* after spending a year in the Yukon Territory in Canada. It is the story of Buck, a domestic dog who becomes wild and eventually leads a wolf pack.

Sensitive ears can track sounds up to 2 miles (3 km) away

Wolves have as many as 17 different facial expressions

Poor eyesight means wolves must rely on superb hearing and sense of smell

Long muzzle hides powerful jaws and teeth capable of killing prey and tearing flesh; 42 teeth include sharp canines, which grip prey

THE WOLF WITHIN
Jack London's novel *White Fang*, set in the Yukon Territory, is the story of a wolf domesticated to become a pet. In practice, it is virtually impossible—and illegal—to keep wild wolves as pets.

Two-layered coat with soft, dense underfur and long, outer hairs keeps out the cold

BORN TO BE WILD
Wolves are well adapted to Arctic life. Their sharp sense of smell and hearing are perfect for tracking down their prey. They have evolved strong bodies and long legs with which they chase down their quarry. Agile and graceful, they can jump up to 15 ft (4.5 m) and can leap upward, sideways, and even backward, like a cat. Just like dogs, wolves walk on their toes and have large pads with claws that do not retract. This allows them to run fast on flat ground while keeping their footing on rocks, ice, and other slippery surfaces.

Wolves can sleep out in the open tundra, although they often find a snow hole or a cave in which to shelter

Gray wolf
Canis lupus

The weighty walrus

HUGE, UNGAINLY, AND ENORMOUSLY FAT, the walrus, a close relative of seals, has adapted superbly to its Arctic lifestyle. A thick layer of blubber (fat) keeps the animal warm. Its four flat flippers make the walrus an excellent swimmer, as well as allow it to shift its heavy bulk on land. Female walruses give birth in the spring, usually on boulder-strewn beaches. The female usually produces one calf every other year and cares for her young for about 2 years—twins are very rare. Walruses follow the seasonal advance and retreat of the Arctic ice, migrating as far as 1,800 miles (3,000 km) north each year. In the process, the animals must evade polar bears and killer whales—their greatest enemies other than humans.

WORLD-FAMOUS WALRUS
Lewis Carroll (1832–98) included a walrus and a carpenter in his famous book *Alice Through the Looking Glass.* They invite some oysters to walk with them and then eat them. In real life, walruses do indeed eat mainly bivalves, such as mussels and clams.

THE CALL OF LOVE
Walrus courtship is an elaborate process. A male seduces a female with barks, growls, and whistles. If she is impressed by his love song, she will slip off with him and mate in the water. These two walruses are tenderly rubbing mustaches prior to mating.

Thick skin on neck and shoulders protects the walrus during fights

FURRY FRIEND
Just like the much smaller catfish, the walruses have a row of coarse but very sensitive whiskers. The whiskers grow constantly to make up for daily wear and tear. The walrus uses the delicate mustache to search for invertebrates on the murky ocean floor.

Broad front flippers can support heavy body on land

Walrus
Odobenus rosmarus

HEAVYWEIGHT
Weighing in at around 2,200 lb (1 metric ton), this formidable male walrus surveys his domain. Females are only slightly smaller, weighing about 1,900 lb (0.85 metric tons).

AN INTIMATE ARRANGEMENT
Walruses are extremely sociable animals. During the summer, bulls and cows lie around on the land, packed together in large, noisy groups called pods. Staying close conserves body heat, as well as making it harder for a predator to pick off an individual animal.

Carved animals decorate the tusk

Cribbage game board carved from a walrus tusk

Walrus ivory is harder than elephant ivory

MULTIPURPOSE ANIMAL
This cribbage board was probably made by a European sailor, but native Inuit people of North America have also always hunted walruses. They, too, carve and decorate the tusks, but they also eat the meat, use the hides for shelter or to make boats, and burn the blubber oil for heat and light.

HEAVE HO!
During the winter and spring, walruses spend much of their time drifting along on large floating fields of ice. They use their tusks as ice picks to heave themselves out of the water, flopping belly down onto the ice.

Heavy skull protects brain when animal smashes through ice up to 9 in (22 cm) thick

Thin layer of body hair is molted (shed) every summer

Blubber may be more than 4 in (10 cm) thick

LONG IN THE TOOTH
A walrus's tusks are actually its upper canine teeth, and they may grow as long as 3 ft (1 m). The walrus perhaps uses its tusks to rake up the sea floor in the search for food. Walruses do not attack humans, but an angry, wounded walrus can injure a hunter and damage his boat when thrashing its head around.

Lower jaw

Walrus can stab larger prey with its tusks, but it eats mainly shellfish

Suited to the sea

SEALS ARE PROBABLY THE HARDIEST of all the Arctic and Antarctic mammals. The ringed seal of the Arctic and the Weddell seal of the Antarctic both survive below the ice during the dark winter months. Other seals, such as the Arctic harp seal, migrate into polar waters as the warmer summer weather arrives. All seals have to leave the water to rest, give birth, and mate. In contrast to their graceful swimming in the sea, seals move clumsily on land, wriggling and sliding across the ice with some difficulty. Seals usually give birth in the late winter. By the spring, the pups are strong enough to start making most of the fish and other rich food supplies of the polar waters. Fur seals and sea lions have problems coping with the heat of an Arctic or Antarctic summer. Their fur and blubber causes them to overheat, and the seals have to pant, flap their flippers, or cover their bodies with sand or mud to cool down. Seals have been hunted for their fur and blubber for hundreds of years; they are also threatened by the increasing pollution of the oceans.

Guard hairs protect the seal as it slides over rocks on land

Dense underfur traps a layer of warm air and keeps seal warm

TWO FUR COATS
Fur seals have two kinds of hair in their coat. Long guard hairs on the outside form a protective layer, and fine underfur keeps body heat from escaping. Other seals have hairless bodies and depend on their blubber for warmth.

ICY WINTERS
Weddell seals (*Leptonychotes weddelli*) spend the whole winter under the Antarctic sea ice, gnawing at the ice with their teeth to keep air holes open for breathing. In the summer, the seals move on to the ice or rocks. Pups are born in September or October and can swim at about 6 weeks. Weddell seals make a wide range of sounds under water, possibly for locating prey or breathing holes or to communicate with other seals. They can dive to depths of about 1,900 ft (580 m) and stay submerged for up to 70 minutes.

BALLOON NOSE
Male hooded seals (*Cystaphora cristata*) of the Arctic have an inflatable balloonlike structure at the end of their nose. The seal inflates it when he is excited or in danger, and it may serve to warn off rivals or enemies.

The male has a huge swollen nose like an elephant's trunk

JOBS FOR THE BOYS
Gigantic male southern elephant seals (*Mirounga leonina*) roar defiance to their rivals in the breeding season, using their extraordinary nose like a loudspeaker. The female gives birth to a single pup, which she nurses for about a month. During this period, she will not feed, existing instead on energy reserves in her blubber. Males do not eat during the breeding season either, since they are constantly defending a harem of females against rival males.

Male elephant seals are up to 10 times heavier than females

While it is nursed, the pup may quadruple its weight in 3–4 weeks

HIDDEN DEATH
Inuit hunters sometimes hide behind white shields mounted on small sleds as they hunt seals.

Cusps on cheek teeth filter food

Cranium

TRIDENT TEETH
The crabeater seal *(Lobodon carcinophagus)* does not eat crabs. It uses its trident-shaped teeth to strain shrimplike krill from Antarctic waters. The crabeater swims at great speed with its mouth open, forcing the water through spaces in its teeth. Between 5–8 million crabeater seals live in the Antarctic; they have few enemies, other than killer whales.

Huge mouth can gape wide open and snap shut to grasp prey

Powerful canine teeth for stripping flesh

Large eyes to find prey underwater

SWIMMING LIMBS
A seal limb looks very different from a human foot. Under the skin, however, the bones are the same, adapted over millions of years to their different functions. A seal limb has been modified to form a webbed paddle. True seals use their back flippers to swim through the water; fur seals and sea lions use their front flippers instead, keeping the back flippers as a rudder for steering.

Tibia

Fibula

Ankle bone

Foot bones

Toe bones

Tibia

Fibula

Ankle bone

Foot bones

Toe bones

Human foot

Seal flipper

SEAL THERAPY
When the strains of underwater life become too much, most seals, such as this leopard seal, hoist themselves up on to the ice for a rest and some sunbathing.

SPOTTED HUNTER
The aggressive leopard seal *(Hydrurga leptonyx)* of the Antarctic is named for the large dark spots on its skin. These slender animals are built for speed and have a long, flexible neck and a wide mouth for grasping penguins, seal pups, and other prey. Leopard seals pursue penguins underwater, then carry their victims to the surface, where they beat them against the water, turning them inside out to remove the skin, before gulping them down. The seal may spend up to an hour slowly eating in this way.

Giants of the seas

INUIT CARVING
This Inuit model of a sperm whale is from Alaska. European whalers were influenced by Inuit carving when they began to engrave the teeth and bones of whales.

T̄HE POLAR SEAS ARE HOME to a whole range of whales. The gray, humpback, fin, and blue whales are summer residents, making good use of a rich supply of plankton. When the winter comes, most of the whales migrate to warmer waters near the equator. The narwhal, beluga, and bowhead whales remain in the Arctic all year round, and minke whales withstand the Antarctic winter. Whales do not feed much during the winter, relying on body fat to sustain them. Whales began to disappear when people hunted them in order to sell their oil, baleen (whalebone), and meat. Now that commercial whaling has declined, many whale populations have recovered.

SEA UNICORN
The spiral tusk of the male narwhal (*Monodon monoceros*) is an elongated tooth. Tusks were traded outside the Arctic before most people had seen narwhals; this may have led to the legend of the unicorn.

Epidermis

Dermis

Blubber can be 10 in (25 cm) thick

Connective tissue

Fascia

Muscles

HOT FAT
Under a whale's skin there is an insulating layer of fatty blubber. A network of blood vessels runs through it. If the whale overheats, more blood is pumped up nearer to the cold water, which cools down the whale.

About 150 pairs of yellowish white baleen plates filter plankton

Blowhole on top of head; nostrils are closed off under water

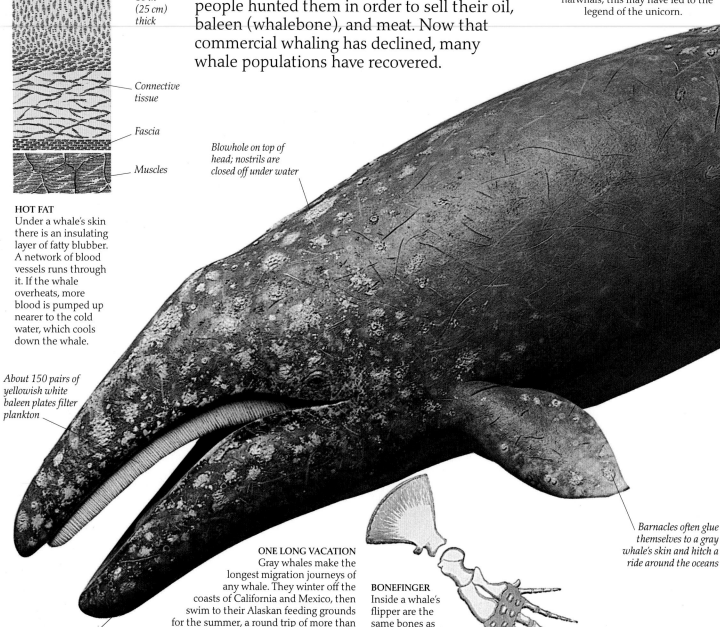

Barnacles often glue themselves to a gray whale's skin and hitch a ride around the oceans

ONE LONG VACATION
Gray whales make the longest migration journeys of any whale. They winter off the coasts of California and Mexico, then swim to their Alaskan feeding grounds for the summer, a round trip of more than 12,000 miles (20,000 km). Gray whales feed only in the summer, living off stores of energy in their blubber for the rest of the year. The young are born in the warmer waters of their winter home.

BONEFINGER
Inside a whale's flipper are the same bones as in our own hands. Flippers are used for steering and braking; the tail provides swimming power.

Two, or sometimes four, grooves on the throat

CHAMPION DIVER
The sperm whale (*Physeter catodon*) can easily dive down to about 1,150 ft (350 m) and stay under for 10 minutes or longer. The longest recorded dive is 90 minutes, and dives occasionally reach 10,000 ft (3,000 m).

CLEVER KILLERS
Killer whales, or orcas (*Orcinus orca*), live in pods of 4–40 individuals that hunt together. They are the fastest mammals in the sea, able to reach 35 mph (56 kph). They even tip seals off ice floes and snatch sea lions from beaches. Nothing is safe from them, not even this bowhead whale.

Back has a row of 6–14 humps, but no dorsal fin

THE BIG ONE
The largest animal that has ever lived, the blue whale (*Balaenoptera musculus*) is longer than a Boeing 737 jet and weighs 25 times more than an African elephant. Blue whales are now rare, since they were brought close to extinction by commercial whaling.

Large, strong muscles in the tail power the flukes. About one-third of a whale's body is pure muscle

Flat, rigid tail flukes, stiffened with cartilage, move up and down to push the whale through the water

Killer whale

Top attaches to the whale's upper jaw

Fish   Seal   Seabird   Minke whale

Squid

NATURAL BALANCE
Killer whales are the top carnivores in many sub-Arctic and sub-Antarctic food chains and are a vital part of the food webs of polar seas. Their prey includes fishes, seals, penguins, and other whales. Fishermen are often in conflict with killer whales because they believe the whales take valuable fish stocks. But the whales are part of the natural balance of life in the oceans, easily upset by people overfishing.

Krill

GIANT FILTERS
Some whales, such as the right whale, gray whale, humpback whale, and blue whale, filter food from the seawater with fringed brushes, called baleen, inside their mouths. These whales have huge, arched jaws from which the baleen plates hang like curtains. Like fingernails, baleen is made of a substance called keratin.

Plankton

A herding life

PEOPLE HAVE SURVIVED in the inhospitable Arctic regions of northern Scandinavia and the northern regions of Siberia for thousands of years. Native Arctic peoples followed a nomadic (traveling) hunting and fishing lifestyle, adapting to the intense winter cold, darkness, and snow without the aid of modern technology. Starvation and death by exposure were constant threats. Native peoples of the Eurasian Arctic include the Saami, or Lapps, of northern Scandinavia, and the Chukchi, Evenks, and Nenets of Siberia and northeastern Asia. Some families still follow wild reindeer herds, hunting or lassoing them for their meat and pelts. Reindeer provided Arctic peoples with all their basic needs—food, clothing, tents, tools, and items to trade. In some remote areas, the native peoples still follow a traditional hunting lifestyle. But many now work in villages or towns, and some combine the old and new ways of life.

Staff is made of iron

SPIRIT POWER
In many traditional Siberian societies, a specially trained *angakok*, or shaman, acted as the link between the supernatural and natural worlds. A shaman fulfilled many roles, from doctor and meteorologist to performer of miracles. This shaman's headdress is embroidered with reindeer hair.

Shaman's head ornament from the Ostyak-Nenet people of Siberia

HANDY IN THE WINTER
This ivory carving of reindeer pulling a sled comes from central Siberia. Many Siberian peoples used reindeer as pack and draft (pulling) animals for carrying their household goods. Today, some reindeer herders hire out their reindeer sleds for transportation during the winter.

Foot represents a bear's paw

Bag is made of stretched reindeer hide

Hide from different parts of the reindeer's body provides the changes of color in the decoration

IN A TRANCE
Shamans of the Tungus people, east of the Yenisey River in central Siberia, held this staff while meditating. The shaman often went into a trance and spoke with the voice of a spirit "helper."

PACK YOUR BAG
The northern Komi live to the west of the Ural Mountains, in northwestern Russia. They filled this *patku*, or knapsack, with clothes and other smaller items and loaded it onto a baggage sled when following reindeer herds.

MOVING CAMP
Because nomadic people often moved several times a year, their tents had to be simple and lightweight as well as sturdy. The tents usually had a conical framework of wooden poles, covered with several reindeer skins. The top of the tent was left open to allow smoke from the fire to escape.

Nenet tent, Siberia

A great deal of heat is lost through the head, so a hood is vital for keeping the head and ears warm in freezing conditions

Seams are very finely stitched to make the garment as warm and waterproof as possible

Nenet child's hooded winter parka

HUNTER OR HUNTED?
This hooded jacket from the Aleutian Islands, between Siberia and Alaska, is made from strips of seal or walrus intestine, sewn together to make a waterproof garment. By dressing in the skins or fur of the animals, the hunter was making an important point—he became part of the animal world around him by taking on the appearance of the hunted.

Reindeer gut was often used for sewing skins together

Mittens are sewn right into the sleeves for extra warmth and protection

Fur trim was decorative, but also protected against icy winds

ORIGINS OF THE PARKA
The traditional winter coat of the Nenet tribe of northern Siberia consisted of a thick, warm long-sleeved jacket called a parka. The coat was sewn together from pieces of reindeer skin. The reindeer hide was worn on the outside; for the inner clothing, softer fur was placed next to the skin for extra warmth. Woolen undergarments provided added protection and helped trap body heat. Some people still wear traditional clothes, but most buy winter clothes made of synthetic materials.

Hunters of the north

The model has a traditional hairstyle

Strips of white hide from underside of caribou are used as decoration

INUIT, INUPIAT, AND YUPIK PEOPLE, called eskimos by 19th-century Europeans, are the original inhabitants of the Arctic tundra of northern Canada, Alaska, Russia, and Greenland. About 100,000 of them still live there. They were nomadic hunter-gatherers. They lived near the coast in the summer, building up food reserves for the winter. The rest of the year, they traveled, hunting caribou, seals, polar bears, and whales, and used every part of the animals they caught for food, shelter, clothing, weapons, and tools. Their society was organized in extended family groups, with each member carrying out a specific job according to sex, age, and status. Games, music, and storytelling helped pass the long winter hours. Most Inuit, Inupiat, and Yupik people now live in permanent settlements, often combining a regular job with hunting trips.

Both men and women wore sealskin boots called kamiks

Inuit clothes were often heavily embroidered

WINTER WARMTH
This traditional man's winter costume is made of caribou skin. Women sewed the skins together with sinew and a bone needle and sometimes decorated the clothes with beadwork or embroidery. Only the families of good hunters replaced their clothes each year. Poor families unable to get caribou skins in the fall wore their clothes for more than a year or had to make their parkas out of sealskins.

ANCIENT ART
Inuit carved elaborate animal figures out of walrus ivory, caribou antlers, and whale or seal bone. They used ivory bow drills as instruments. This Inuit carving of a woman standing on a seal comes from Baffin Island. Today, Inuit artists use modern tools and soapstone to make carvings for tourists.

Only the tiniest area is exposed to the freezing air

Hunter pulled on line attached to harpoon to haul seal out of the water

Fitted tray holds leather harpoon rope

Sealskin jacket protected hunter from icy Arctic winds

A seal bladder float was attached to any large catch so that it would float behind the canoe

MASK

Inuit art, such as this wooden mask, often reflected the supernatural world and the activities of the shamans. Only a shaman would have worn a mask like this, but the Inuit also made a variety of small bone and soapstone maskettes for rituals and ceremonies. They also made carvings of abstract shapes and of natural objects such as animals.

Slit for eye

Mask was held on by leather straps that ran through holes at the side

Shaman's wooden mask, Barrow Point

Woodworms, which do not exist in Arctic temperatures, have pitted this mask since its collection for a museum

SHORT-LIVED SEAL

Some Inuit copied polar bears in their hunting techniques, catching seals at their breathing holes in the winter ice. Dogs were used to sniff out the breathing hole if it had become covered by snow. When the seal emerged, the hunter thrust in his harpoon, pulled out the seal, and dragged it to his sled.

Animal carvings were believed to give a hunter special powers

TOOL FOR THE JOB

Like the seal-hunting peoples of the Artic, the Haida people of the Pacific coast of Canada hunted seals with carved wooden clubs. The Inuit respected the animals they hunted. They beheaded animals they killed to release their spirits and often returned a small part of a sea mammal to the ocean to encourage rebirth.

Boat is covered with sealskin

Light wooden paddle for rowing through ice

Sharply pointed harpoon

KAYAK

The Inuit used kayaks to hunt sea mammals such as seals and whales. Kayaks were one-man hunting craft, completely enclosed except for an opening for the hunter to climb in at the top. Umiaks were larger, open, hide-covered boats used for transporting goods and people, and also for hunting whales.

Discovering the Arctic

From the 15th century, European powers, intent on trade expansion, sponsored voyages into uncharted waters. Much of the early European exploration was centered on the search for a northern sea route to China and India, which would halve the time and danger involved in traveling overland. After the discovery of America, two routes were envisioned: the Northwest Passage, following the American coast, and the Northeast Passage, along the Siberian coast. The search for the Northwest Passage was soon monopolized by the British and the French but was later joined by the Americans; the Dutch and the Russians concentrated on the northeast. Over the next 350 years, explorers opened up the Arctic, but it was not until 1878 that a Swede, Adolf Nordenskjïld, navigated the Northeast Passage, and 1905 when the great Norwegian explorer Roald Amundsen sailed through the Northwest Passage.

UP AND AWAY
Salomon Andrée, a Swedish aeronaut, and two companions tried to reach the North Pole in the balloon Örnen (*Eagle*) in 1897. The balloon was weighed down by ice and forced to land. All three men perished.

Sir John Franklin 1786–1847

Fox collar

RESCUE FOXES
Eight foxes were released in the Canadian Arctic wearing collars bearing the name and position of a rescue ship, and medals were distributed among the local people. It was hoped they might encounter Franklin survivors.

Medal

THE SEARCHERS
In 1845, Sir John Franklin led 128 men on a search for the Northwest Passage. By 1847, nothing had been heard from them, and his wife mobilized many expeditions to hunt for them. In fact, they had all died, but the searches greatly advanced geographical knowledge of the Arctic.

THE HOMECOMING
In 1818, John Ross (leading the procession) returned home to England, having failed to find the Northwest Passage but having succeeded in killing a bear! This cartoon was by George Cruickshank.

Small slits let in
minimum glare

Sails made of
strong canvas

SNOW BLINDNESS

The rays of the Arctic sun shining on snow are dazzling. The light can cause temporary blindness and may damage the eyes. Arctic peoples fashioned goggles from leather or occasionally wood. Early explorers followed their example. These goggles belonged to Sir William Parry, who had traveled far north in search of the Northwest Passage and was later one of the searchers for Sir John Franklin's ill-fated expedition.

THE PASSAGE SAILED

In 1903, aboard an old fishing boat called the *Gjoa* loaded with three years' provisions, the Norwegian explorer Roald Amundsen and six companions set out to navigate the Northwest Passage. On the way, they spent two years on King William Island studying the Inuit way of life and collecting scientific data. In 1905, the *Gjoa* set off again and reached the Pacific. Fifty years earlier, between 1850–54, Captain Robert McClure and his crew had made the journey east to west, doing the central part of it on foot after losing their ship, but Amundsen was the first to sail through.

*Chocolate was left in
Canada by Sir James Ross's
expedition in 1849*

*Dried biscuit
was staple fare*

Two larger boats
were carried, as well
as the small lifeboat

Tripe de roche

Auxiliary engine
fitted to the ship

Small lifeboat

Barrels
containing
water

FOOD FAILURE

Many expeditions failed because the food supplies taken were either inadequate or insufficient in quantity. The value of carbohydrates was not known, and many explorers suffered from scurvy through lack of vitamin C. Explorers tried to utilize natural resources like *tripe de roche*, a kind of lichen, on which Captain Parry's sailors lived in 1824.

Race for the pole

Surveying the land

AT THE BEGINNING of the 20th century, several nations wanted to explore the Antarctic. In 1910, British adventurer Robert Falcon Scott (1868–1912) set out for the South Pole. His expedition had scientific objectives. After using motorized sleds, ponies, and dogs, and then hauling their own sleds through the harsh terrain, Scott and four companions, Wilson, Bowers, Oates, and Evans, finally arrived at the pole only to find that Norwegian explorer Roald Amundsen had reached it weeks before them. On the return journey the weather worsened, and weakened by cold and hunger, all five men perished. But, although they lost the polar race, their scientific studies greatly advanced Antarctic science.

RUNNING REPAIRS
Dr. Wilson took this sewing kit on the ill-fated 1910–12 expedition. Keeping cotton and canvas clothing in good repair was essential in the harsh and difficult conditions.

Compact and lightweight kit for traveling

Microscope magnifies the image inside the instrument

Side mirror reflects light into the instrument

Günther & Tegetmeyer BRAUNSCHWEIG, NO 4716

BASE CAMP
From this desk in his "den" in base camp at Cape Evans, Scott wrote his diary, letters, and reports, studied maps, and planned the details of his trek to the pole. The extreme cold and the dry atmosphere have preserved the hut virtually as it was in 1910.

ELECTRIC SPIDER
This electrometer, taken by Scott to Antarctica, was used to measure tiny fluctuations in atmospheric electricity. If there was a difference in electric charge between the Earth and the atmosphere, a small suspended mirror inside the electrometer would move. This movement was compared against the fixed line of a suspended fine filament from a black widow spider's web.

Wire to ground the instrument

54

String attached compass to a steady point

SUN ROUTE
This compass was used on Scott's 1910 expedition. From the time on a watch and the known position of the Sun in the sky at that time, explorers could figure out a north–south direction using the compass and a chronometer.

POCKET HOSPITAL
A tiny medical kit was an essential part of polar expeditions. Injuries and frostbite had to be treated quickly in the harsh conditions.

Tablets of painkillers such as morphine and cocaine

NEW LIFE
The *Terra Nova*, the ship in which Scott sailed to Antarctica on his last expedition, was originally a Scottish whaling vessel. Scott sailed to Cape Evans on Ross Island and set up his base camp there.

Poisons such as strychnine were used for medicinal purposes

Syringe for administering standard doses of medicine

THE "TERRA NOVA"

Instrument made mostly of brass so not affected by magnetic fields

LAST BASE
This pile of rocks marks the spot where the bodies of Scott, Wilson, and Bowers are buried. Only 11 miles (18 km) from a food depot, they were exhausted from hauling supplies and over 35 lb (15 kg) of geological specimens.

First to the pole

The Norwegian explorer Roald Amundsen (1872–1928) chose a different route to the pole than Scott. He also started his journey closer to the pole than Scott, setting up base camp at Framheim on the Ross Ice Shelf. Amundsen's expedition was better prepared and organized for fast travel than Scott's. They also took along more food. His polar party consisted of expert skiers and navigators and relied heavily on their dogs for both transportation, and later, as food.

FLYING THE FLAG
Amundsen set out for the South Pole on October 20, 1911, across the previously unexplored Axel Heiberg glacier. He reached the pole on December 14, beating Scott by just over a month. Amundsen also made several expeditions to the Arctic, flying over the North Pole in the airship *Norge* in 1926. He was lost in a rescue mission in the Arctic in 1928.

ANTARCTICA

South Pole
Transantarctic Mountains
Ross Ice Shelf
Scott's last camp
Framheim
Cape Evans
Ross Sea

Amundsen's route
Scott's route

Staying warm and safe

FIGURE OF FUR
Amundsen's clothing was typical of that worn in the early 1900s.

EARLY EXPLORERS SUFFERED greatly because they did not know how to stay warm and, equally important, dry, in harsh conditions. The freezing power of the icy winds was also largely ignored. Frostbite was very common, and many men died of exposure. In time, lessons were learned from the native peoples, and by the early years of this century, equipment had improved enormously. Explorers used sleeping bags and fur boots and wore canvas jackets to protect themselves from the icy winds. Bringing the right food supplies was extremely important. On many early expeditions, too much emphasis was placed on the need for meat, and carbohydrates, vital for energy, were largely ignored. Today, a great deal is known about the foods necessary for a healthy diet.

LAYER BY LAYER
The inadequacy of the clothes they wore contributed to the deaths of Captain Scott and his companions. They sweated a lot—the sweat froze, making the body cold and the clothes heavy and uncomfortable. Layers of lightweight clothes would have allowed good ventilation with the trapped air insulating against the cold.

Polypropylene fabric takes moisture away from the body, preventing heat loss caused by sweat evaporation

Inner layer: "long johns" worn next to the skin

Potato

Bolognese sauce   Shepherd's pie

Cooking vessel

Removable inner sole

TRAVELING LIGHT
Traveling in the freezing polar landscapes is hard work, whether on skis or by snowmobile or sled. Therefore, food has to be light and compact and quick and easy to prepare. Dried foods that only have to be mixed with heated ice or snow fulfill all the requirements and are also nutritious.

Thermal lining can be removed for easy drying

Padded sole for extra toughness

FEET FIRST
The feet and the hands are especially vulnerable to frostbite, so it is essential that these parts of the body are adequately covered. Today, different types of footwear have been designed for different conditions.

Glacier boots for use in deep powder snow

Adjustable lacing ensures a good fit

Thick, ridged rubber soles help prevent slipping

EYE SHADES
Goggles are worn to protect eyes from windblown snow and the glare of sunlight reflected off snow and ice.

Middle layer: fiberpile undergarment traps a layer of air, which is warmed by the body

ICE CRACKER
When climbing steep ice, two ice axes are hammered into the ice face. The climber then uses them to pull himself up.

Zippers allow garments to be easily removed

Waterproof nylon covering keeps the goosedown from becoming wet and losing insulating efficiency

Outer layer: jacket

Adjustable wrists prevent snow from entering mitt

Thermal inner mitts are worn alone for delicate outside work

Waterproof outer mitts are lined with fiberpile fabric for warmth

POLAR MAN
One of the many advantages of layer dressing is that the number of layers can be adjusted according to the activity of the wearer and the temperature. This outer layer, consisting of jacket and pants, is filled with pure high-quality goosedown, which is the most efficient of natural fillings. Combined with the mid and base layers, these garments provide insulation sufficient to keep warm at -40° F (-40° C).

Outer layer: thick, padded pants

Crampons attached to the soles provide grip

FOOT SUPPORT
These climbing boots are made of strong and fairly stiff plastic that supports the foot and ankle. They have a removable thermal lining.

Thermal socks worn next to the skin

Padded socks add extra warmth and help keep the feet dry

Polar travel

THE FIRST SNOWMOBILE
Scott's motorized sled was the first vehicle with caterpillar tracks to be designed especially for snow. The slats on the tracks helped to grip the snow. The vehicle was far ahead of its time, but it had an unreliable early gasoline engine and soon developed serious mechanical faults in the severe Antarctic environment. But it was a forerunner of the snowmobiles of today.

THE SNOW AND ICE of polar regions have always posed special problems for travelers. Snowshoes and skis keep people from sinking too far into soft snow, and boots with rough or spiked soles grip icy ground. Long, low sleds on smooth runners reduce friction and make it easier to move heavy loads over slippery, frozen surfaces. Early polar explorers learned from native Arctic peoples the benefits of using husky dogs to pull sleds. (Nomadic Lapp people used reindeer for the same purpose.) Modern motorized vehicles, such as the snowcat, with clawlike grips, or the snowmobile, with skis underneath, were developed from tried and tested traditional forms of transportation.

POLAR HORSESHOE
The pressure of a horse's or pony's hooves drives straight down through the snow, causing them to sink up to their bellies. The hooves also break through sea ice and snow bridges very easily. Snowshoes for horses and ponies help spread out the weight so they have more chance of staying on the surface.

Tennis racket shape to spread weight as evenly as possible

A BRAVE MAN'S SHOES
These snowshoes were worn by Captain Oates, who perished on Scott's 1910–12 expedition to Antarctica. Oates's feet became frostbitten on the return journey, and then gangrenous. Rather than hold up his companions, he walked out of Scott's tent in a blizzard to die, so that they would be free to press on as fast as possible. His last words were: "I am just going outside and may be some time." He hoped that this would enable his companions to save themselves, but tragically, his heroic gesture did not have the result he desired.

TOBOGGAN RUN
Sleds used in the Arctic and Antarctic need to be strong enough to carry heavy loads, but light enough for dogs or people to pull. Different types of sled suit different conditions. Narrow runners are best for hard ice; wide runners are best for soft snow. This wooden sled dates from 1934–37 and is loaded with scientific equipment, food, and medical supplies. A team of 12 huskies can pull a fully loaded sled weighing half a ton.

Shovel for digging snow

Wooden runners reinforced with iron on the base

Flat-bottomed sled like a toboggan "floats" easily over the surface of the snow without sinking in too far

A RARE SIGHT
When Lapp people lived as nomads, migrating from place to place, they used reindeer as pack animals or to pull sleds. Today they rarely do so, because most Lapp families have settled in villages, although they still keep reindeer.

CANOEING THE SNOW
Traditional methods of travel in Lapland included various types of canoe-shaped sled called *pulkka*. These had one runner only and were usually pulled by reindeer. A common kind of *pulkka* was large enough for one adult passenger, who sat with his legs outstretched, ready for braking. A wider *pulkka* was used to transport belongings. A third kind of *pulkka* was used by the Skolt Lapps for carrying sick people, children, and belongings. Reindeer were harnessed three abreast to this *pulkka*.

SMOOTH MOVERS
These heavy wooden skis were used by Scott on his first expedition to Antarctica in 1901–04. Skis can be used on most kinds of snow and ice. They spread out the weight of a person, helping them stay on the surface of the snow. They also reduce friction, sliding easily over snow and ice and allowing greater distances to be covered than by walking.

SNOW DOGS
The husky dogs used to pull sleds are social animals, working in a strict hierarchy under their leader in the sled team. They are hardy, strong, and intelligent, but compulsive fighters. Huskies can survive freezing temperatures curled up in snowdrifts. The snow acts as an insulating blanket, helping keep them warm at night or during blizzards.

Stout wooden cases loaded with scientific equipment, food, and medical supplies

Canvas cover for protecting supplies

"WITH CAPTAIN SCOTT AT THE SOUTH POLE"
Fry's PURE **Cocoa** & CHOCOLATE

MAKERS TO H. M. THE KING.

DRIVEN TO THE DOGS
Sleds pulled by dogs are one of the best means of moving heavy loads over ice and snow. Usually, it takes at least a year or two of hard practice to learn how to drive a dog sled.

Life at the poles

T HE CRUEL SEAS, savage and unpredictable climates, and inhospitable terrains of the two polar regions have ensured that neither environment has ever been completely conquered by humans. The history of polar exploration is one of appalling hardship and terrible toll of human life. However, in the Arctic, the Inuit peoples evolved survival skills over the centuries that enabled them to live a fruitful existence. European explorers learned much from their way of life and gradually applied this knowledge to their own ability to explore and live in these harsh environments. Today, the lifestyle at the poles for both Inuit and other polar dwellers is very similar. Scientific advances in clothing, transportation, food, and building have ensured a way of life far removed from the hardships of earlier times.

HELPING HANDS
Many early explorers died because they could not build strong enough shelters. By the 19th century, Arctic explorers realized how much they could learn from the native peoples.

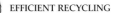

EFFICIENT RECYCLING
On Scott's last expedition, Edward Wilson made a successful candlestick out of a cracker box. Explorers tried to find an alternative use for everything.

Window made from a block of freshwater ice

Entrance passage

Storage alcove

OVERNIGHT STAY
Today, some Inuit still build igloos as temporary shelter. Here, this hunter is lighting his primus stove, with which he will warm himself and cook his dinner.

SNOW HOUSE
Contrary to popular belief, Inuit never built igloos as permanent homes, but as temporary bases during the winter seal-hunting season. For much of the time, they lived partly underground in dwellings made on a frame of driftwood or whalebone and covered by grass.

Gas shaft

Office block housing specialized scientific areas

Main access shaft

Garage

Library

Lounge

Dormitory block

Kitchen

Dining room

Sled stores

Infirmary; most illnesses are treated at the station

Halley IV, 1983–92

ALL MODERN CONVENIENCES

Today, several countries have temporary or permanent research stations in the Antarctic. They carry out scientific work in geology, geophysics, biology, and atmospheric sciences. Some bases, like this historic version of Britain's Halley Station, are built on top of ice shelves, where they are buried by 3 ft (1 m) of snow per year and eventually crushed. The latest version of Halley Station (Halley VI) is on stilts and can be jacked up to stay above the rising snow.

SKIDDING AROUND

Polar travel is no longer reliant on dogs or ponies. Today, most people travel on snowmobiles, which are small motorized sleds on skis. They are easy to maneuver and pull very heavy loads.

Blubber oil lamp

Women wear leather inner garments

Wooden sleeping platform covered with furs

LAB OF THE NORTH

Canada has several research laboratories in the Arctic. This space-age laboratory at Igloolik in Canada's Northwest Territories has contributed much to scientific knowledge of the Arctic region.

Frame for drying skins

Harpoons for hunting seal

Domino-shaped blocks of frozen snow

Last frontiers

GARBAGE DISPOSAL
The way people dispose of their trash in the Arctic and Antarctic often pollutes or damages the environment. Garbage dumps on the edge of Churchill, Canada, attract polar bears, which can be poisoned or injured by eating the garbage. The bears' nearness also causes fears for people's safety.

At THE HEIGHT OF SUMMER in the Antarctic, tourist ships move gently around the coast. In the past, such sights would have been unthinkable, but today people are willing to pay large amounts of money to see the last real wilderness in the world. In the Arctic, careless human exploitation in the past has damaged the fragile ecosystem. Today, concerned governments are trying to find ways to develop the region while caring for the very special natural environment. Because the Antarctic is less accessible than the Arctic, it is still largely undamaged by humans, although holes in the ozone layer above the Antarctic have already been discovered. Many people believe that one way to preserve the area is to make the whole region into a world park, with every form of exploitation internationally banned. It is important to conserve the Arctic and Antarctic so that future generations can experience these extraordinary environments with their unique wildlife in their natural state.

DAY TRIPPERS
Tourist visits to the Antarctic have to be carefully monitored and organized, as tourists could damage fragile vegetation and disturb nesting and breeding grounds. On the other hand, tourist visits can help spread concern for conservation.

All snowflakes have six points

LANDS OF SNOW
The permanence of snow and ice in the Arctic and Antarctic is what makes these regions unique. Snow reflects the Sun's rays, helping keep temperatures low at all times.

Copper on limonite

Dendritic copper

Crystals angled in random growth directions

Lines of striations formed as the crystal grew

Well-developed crystal faces

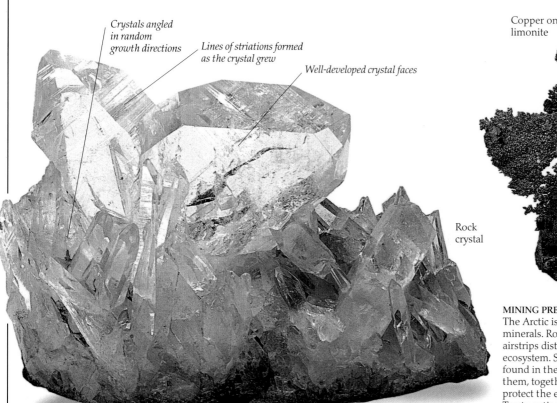

Rock crystal

Limonite groundmass

MINING PRESSURE
The Arctic is mined for oil, coal, and other minerals. Roads, mines, ports, pipelines, and airstrips disturb wildlife and damage the fragile ecosystem. Several minerals have already been found in the Antarctic, but the costs of exploiting them, together with increasing pressure to protect the environment, have led the Antarctic Treaty nations to agree to ban mining until 2041.

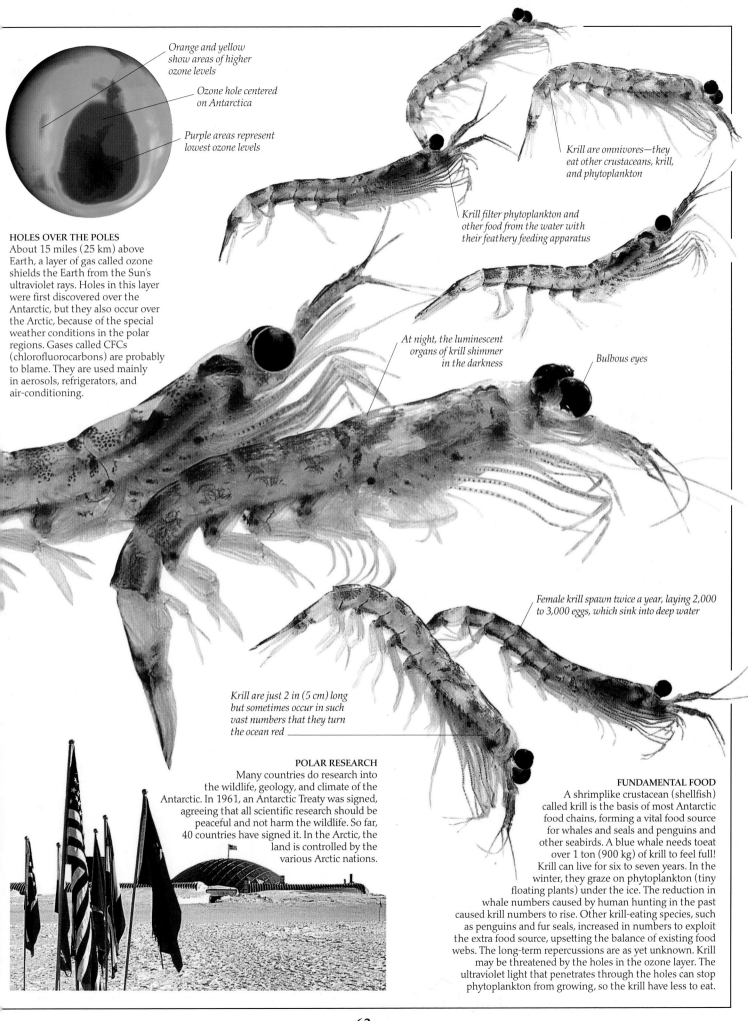

Orange and yellow show areas of higher ozone levels

Ozone hole centered on Antarctica

Purple areas represent lowest ozone levels

HOLES OVER THE POLES

About 15 miles (25 km) above Earth, a layer of gas called ozone shields the Earth from the Sun's ultraviolet rays. Holes in this layer were first discovered over the Antarctic, but they also occur over the Arctic, because of the special weather conditions in the polar regions. Gases called CFCs (chlorofluorocarbons) are probably to blame. They are used mainly in aerosols, refrigerators, and air-conditioning.

Krill are omnivores—they eat other crustaceans, krill, and phytoplankton

Krill filter phytoplankton and other food from the water with their feathery feeding apparatus

At night, the luminescent organs of krill shimmer in the darkness

Bulbous eyes

Female krill spawn twice a year, laying 2,000 to 3,000 eggs, which sink into deep water

Krill are just 2 in (5 cm) long but sometimes occur in such vast numbers that they turn the ocean red

POLAR RESEARCH

Many countries do research into the wildlife, geology, and climate of the Antarctic. In 1961, an Antarctic Treaty was signed, agreeing that all scientific research should be peaceful and not harm the wildlife. So far, 40 countries have signed it. In the Arctic, the land is controlled by the various Arctic nations.

FUNDAMENTAL FOOD

A shrimplike crustacean (shellfish) called krill is the basis of most Antarctic food chains, forming a vital food source for whales and seals and penguins and other seabirds. A blue whale needs to eat over 1 ton (900 kg) of krill to feel full! Krill can live for six to seven years. In the winter, they graze on phytoplankton (tiny floating plants) under the ice. The reduction in whale numbers caused by human hunting in the past caused krill numbers to rise. Other krill-eating species, such as penguins and fur seals, increased in numbers to exploit the extra food source, upsetting the balance of existing food webs. The long-term repercussions are as yet unknown. Krill may be threatened by the holes in the ozone layer. The ultraviolet light that penetrates through the holes can stop phytoplankton from growing, so the krill have less to eat.

Mapping Antarctica

ANTARCTICA IS A HUGE ISOLATED CONTINENT almost entirely covered by ice, where no plants can grow. The thickness of the ice means that on average, its surface is the highest of all the world's continents. Currents and strong winds sweep around the surrounding oceans, acting as a natural barrier between Antarctica and the rest of the world and helping keep it much colder than the Arctic. Cold sea water also drifts northward from the continent, so that its cooling influence extends far beyond the Antarctic Circle. The southernmost Atlantic, Pacific, and Indian oceans together form what is sometimes called the Southern Ocean, surrounding Antarctica. Islands in this ocean provide breeding grounds for millions of seabirds attracted by the Antarctic's marine riches.

Key to map symbols

- ● Capital city
- ○ Settlement
- ◉ Scientific research station
- △ Mountain
-   Glacier
- ···· Average limit of continuous sea ice
- ···· Limit of summer pack ice
- ···· Limit of winter pack ice
- → Warm current
- → Cold current
-   Tundra

ATLANTIC OCEAN

INDIAN OCEAN

PACIFIC OCEAN

Antarctic Circle

Orcadas (Argentina)
South Orkney Islands
Signy (UK)
South Shetland Islands
Esperanza (Argentina)
Capitán Arturo Prat (Chile)
Palmer (US)
Rothera (UK)
San Martin (Argentina)

Drake Passage

Antarctic Peninsula
Graham Land
Palmer Land

Weddell Sea

Halley (UK)

Sanae (South Africa)
Georg von Neumayer (Germany)
Novolazarevskaya (Russian Federation)
Lützow Holmbukta

Dronning Maud Land

Syowa (Japan)
Molodezhnaya (Russian Federation)

Enderby Land

Coats Land
Belgrano II (Argentina)
Berkner Island
Ronne Ice Shelf

Mawson (Australia)

Cape Darnley
Mackenzie Bay
Prydz Bay
Princess Elizabeth Land
Davis (Australia)

Average limit of continuous sea ice
Limit of summer pack ice

ANTARCTICA

East Antarctica

Bellingshausen Sea

Ellsworth Land

△ Vinson Massif 16,066 ft (4,897 m)

West Antarctica

+ Amundsen-Scott (US)
+ South Pole

PETER I ISLAND (to Norway)

Marie Byrd Land

Transantarctic Mountains

Mount Kirkpatrick 14,855 ft (4,528 m) △
Mount Markham 14,275 ft (4,351 m) △

Mirny (Russ. Fed.)
Shackleton Ice Shelf

Vostok (Russian Federation)

Amundsen Sea

△ Mount Sidley 13,717 ft (4,181 m)

Mount Siple △ 10,171 ft (3,100 m)

Roosevelt Island

Ross Ice Shelf

Wilkes Land

Casey (Australia)

Cape Poinsett

Ross Sea
McMurdo Base (US)
Scott Base (NZ)
Mount Erebus 12,447 ft (3,794 m)

Victoria Land

Terre Adélie

Cape Adare

George V Land

Dumont d'Urville (France)

South Geomagnetic Pole +

Limit of summer pack ice
Limit of winter pack ice

Leningradskaya (Russian Federation)

Balleny Islands

0 km   500
0 miles   500

Mapping the Arctic

THE ARCTIC IS LESS ISOLATED than the Antarctic, since the northern continents extend well inside the Arctic Circle. Much of the deep Arctic Ocean is covered by permanent pack ice, which is slowly rotated by ocean currents. The biggest area of land ice, though much smaller than Antarctica, is the Greenland Ice Sheet. Warm currents from the Atlantic Ocean mean that the Arctic seas north of Europe stay more free of ice than elsewhere.

EXTREME SEASONS
The poles experience extreme seasons due to the Earth's tilt toward the Sun. Earth spins at an angle, so whether the North or South pole is tilted toward the Sun depends on the time of year. The diagram above shows the southern midsummer, when the whole area within the Antarctic Circle is receiving 24-hour daylight, while the Arctic lies in winter darkness.

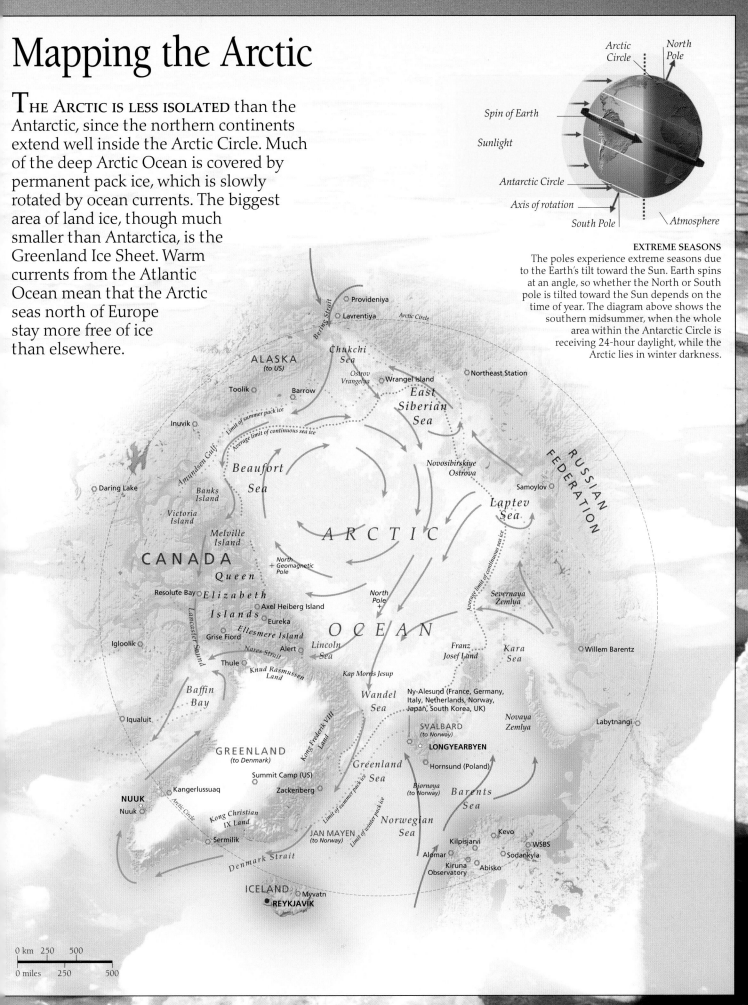

Arctic Circle
North Pole
Spin of Earth
Sunlight
Antarctic Circle
Axis of rotation
South Pole
Atmosphere

Provideniya
Lavrentiya
Arctic Circle
Chukchi Sea
ALASKA (to US)
Ostrov Vrangelya
Wrangel Island
Northeast Station
East Siberian Sea
Toolik
Barrow
Inuvik
Limit of summer pack ice
Average limit of continuous sea ice
Novosibirskiye Ostrova
Samoylov
RUSSIAN FEDERATION
Amundsen Gulf
Beaufort Sea
Daring Lake
Banks Island
Laptev Sea
Victoria Island
Melville Island
A R C T I C
North Geomagnetic Pole
Severnaya Zemlya
CANADA
Queen
Resolute Bay
Elizabeth
North Pole
O C E A N
Axel Heiberg Island
Eureka
Islands
Ellesmere Island
Grise Fiord
Igloolik
Alert
Lincoln Sea
Franz Josef Land
Kara Sea
Willem Barentz
Nares Strait
Lancaster Sound
Thule
Knud Rasmussen Land
Kap Morris Jesup
Baffin Bay
Wandel Sea
Ny-Ålesund (France, Germany, Italy, Netherlands, Norway, Japan, South Korea, UK)
Novaya Zemlya
Labytnangi
Iqaluit
SVALBARD (to Norway)
LONGYEARBYEN
Kong Frederik VIII Land
GREENLAND (to Denmark)
Greenland Sea
Hornsund (Poland)
Summit Camp (US)
Zackenberg
Bjørnøya (to Norway)
Barents Sea
NUUK
Nuuk
Arctic Circle
Kangerlussuaq
Kong Christian IX Land
Limit of summer pack ice
Norwegian Sea
Kevo
WSBS
Sermilik
JAN MAYEN (to Norway)
Limit of winter pack ice
Kilpisjärvi
Alomar
Sodankyla
Denmark Strait
Kiruna Observatory
Abisko
ICELAND
Myvatn
REYKJAVIK

0 km 250 500
0 miles 250 500

Climate—past and future

Polar climates have been changing ever since Earth was formed. Twenty million years ago, there was no ice at all in the polar regions. But, 20,000 years ago, Earth was in the grip of an ice age. Ice cores drilled from polar ice sheets show us records of these fluctuations on Earth and of changes in the atmosphere. We are now in a period of rapid warming, which seems to be caused by such changes. The effects of warming could be dramatic—on both the polar regions and the rest of the world.

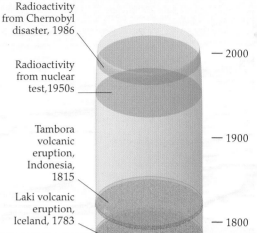

Radioactivity from Chernobyl disaster, 1986

Radioactivity from nuclear test,1950s

Tambora volcanic eruption, Indonesia, 1815

Laki volcanic eruption, Iceland, 1783

ICE CORE ANALYSIS

The Greenland ice sheet has built up over thousands of years. It is made of compressed snow, which contains tiny bubbles of air that were trapped when it formed. These trapped bubbles can record air pollution and gases in the atmosphere, while the ice can record hanging temperatures. Scientists drill down into the ice and extract long ice cores for analysis. This diagram of a 1,000-year ice core from the Greenland ice sheet shows how it records events in the atmosphere over long time periods.

Little ice age—series of cold periods in Northern Hemisphere, 1450–1850

Orefajokull volcanic eruption, Iceland, 1362

— 2000
— 1900
— 1800
— 1700
— 1600
— 1500
— 1400
— 1300
— 1200
— 1100
— 1000 CE

ICE CORE

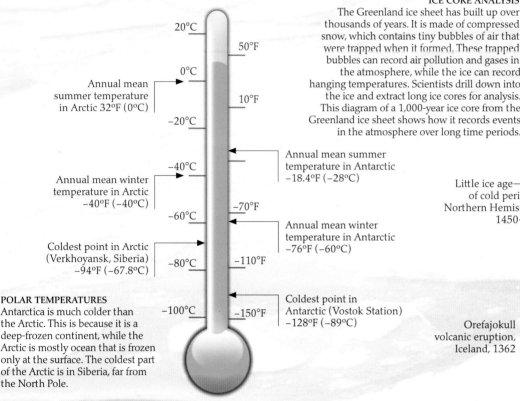

20°C
0°C
−20°C
−40°C
−60°C
−80°C
−100°C

50°F
10°F
−70°F
−110°F
−150°F

Annual mean summer temperature in Arctic 32°F (0°C)

Annual mean winter temperature in Arctic −40°F (−40°C)

Coldest point in Arctic (Verkhoyansk, Siberia) −94°F (−67.8°C)

Annual mean summer temperature in Antarctic −18.4°F (−28°C)

Annual mean winter temperature in Antarctic −76°F (−60°C)

Coldest point in Antarctic (Vostok Station) −128°F (−89°C)

POLAR TEMPERATURES

Antarctica is much colder than the Arctic. This is because it is a deep-frozen continent, while the Arctic is mostly ocean that is frozen only at the surface. The coldest part of the Arctic is in Siberia, far from the North Pole.

Carbon dioxide in the atmosphere
(from the Vostok ice core)

400,000 350,000 300,000 250,000 200,000 150,000 100,000 50,000 0

Temperature change
(from the Vostok ice core)

°C
4
2
0
−2
−4
−6
−8
−10

°F
7.2
3.6
0
−3.6
−7.2
−10.8
−14.4
−18.0

400,000 350,000 300,000 250,000 200,000 150,000 100,000 50,000 0

Years before 1950

CARBON DIOXIDE

The center of the Antarctic ice sheet is known as the Vostok ice core. It has a record of changes in the atmosphere over at least 400,000 years. It shows that carbon dioxide (CO_2) levels have fluctuated since that time. Air samples since 1950 show much higher levels of this gas.

TEMPERATURE

The ice in an ice core records changes in the local air temperature. The changes in temperature over the last 400,000 years match the fluctuations in carbon dioxide recorded in the same ice core. Since carbon dioxide in the air helps keep the planet warm, higher levels of this gas lead to higher temperatures.

Larsen Ice Shelf in 1992, prior to the collapse in 1995

SEA ICE

Rising global temperatures are having a serious effect on the floating ice that forms on polar oceans. The Arctic sea ice is only half as thick as it was in 1960. Since 1979, the size of the frozen ocean in summer has shrunk by about 600,000 sq miles (1.5 million sq km)—an area twice the size of Texas, US. In the winter, the ice sheet doubles in size. But the chart above shows that even the winter ice is shrinking. Each year is different, but the trend is down.

GREENHOUSE EFFECTS

• Earth's atmosphere acts as insulation that stops heat from escaping into space. Without it, the average global temperature would be 54°F (30°C) lower, the oceans would freeze, and life would be impossible. The insulation is called the greenhouse effect.

• The greenhouse effect is caused by certain gases in the atmosphere that absorb heat radiated by the planet. These "greenhouse gases" include carbon dioxide, methane, and nitrous oxide.

• If more carbon dioxide or other greenhouse gases are added to the atmosphere, they increase the greenhouse effect. As a result, the atmosphere retains more heat. This raises global temperatures.

• Air samples show that carbon dioxide levels in the air have been rising steadily since 1958. Climate records show that average global temperatures have been increasing at the same rate.

• It is likely that the rising temperatures are caused by the extra carbon dioxide in the air. This is released by burning coal, oil, and natural gas to fuel transportation and generate electricity. The more fuel we burn, the more carbon dioxide is released, causing climate change.

Larsen Ice Shelf in 1997, after the collapse in 1995

LARSEN ICE SHELF COMPARISON

The fringes of Antarctica are warming up faster than anywhere else on Earth. Average temperatures on the Antarctic Peninsula, near South America, have risen by up to 5.4°F (3°C) since 1951. The land here was once bordered by a floating ice shelf divided into three parts—Larsen A, B, and C. In 1995, Larsen A—on the left of this satellite image—broke up and the ice drifted away as icebergs, which eventually melted. In early 2002, the same happened to Larsen B, on the right. Ice shelves like these support the edges of the vast Antarctic ice sheets, and their collapse could have serious consequences.

RISING SEA LEAVEL

This tiny island community is one of 280 inhabited coral islands in the Maldives, in the Indian Ocean. On average, the islands lie just 5 ft (1.5 m) above the waves. So any rise in sea level is a serious problem. The melting polar ice sheets are pouring vast amounts of meltwater into the warming oceans. The waves are already surging farther inland at high tide. They swamp houses on some islands, and contaminate freshwater supplies. Some scientists predict that global levels could rise by 35 in (88 cm) by the end of the century, which would be disastrous for the Maldives. But no one knows exactly when and how the polar ice sheets will melt. If they collapse suddenly, far more ice will slip into the sea, and coastal cities from New York, US to Shanghai, China could be under threat.

Species status

POLAR ANIMALS ARE GENERALLY doing well compared with wildlife elsewhere, but they still face many challenges. Whale populations remain much reduced after past hunting. On oceanic islands, introduced rats and cats pose a threat to the seabirds that nest there. Many animals depend on sea ice for shelter or hunting. But global warming is melting sea ice, and there is some evidence that it will continue to do so. For marine mammals and birds, other problems include food shortages because humans catch their fish prey. They also face a risk of becoming entangled in fishing gear themselves.

EMPEROR PENGUIN

Scientific name:
Aptenodytes forsteri

Location: Antarctica, breeding on sea ice attached to the mainland

Additional breeding colonies of emperor penguins have been discovered in recent years in Antarctica, boosting the known population of this still-thriving species. There are around 200,000 breeding pairs on Antarctic ice shelves.

ARCTIC FOX

Scientific name: *Alopex lagopus*

Location: Tundra regions all around the Arctic

The Arctic fox is protected in Scandinavia, where numbers are low. These versatile foxes are widespread in the rest of the Arctic and are not considered threatened overall.

BLACK-BROWED ALBATROSS

Scientific name: *Thalassarche melanophrys*

Location: Breed on sub-Antarctic islands all around the Southern Ocean

There are an estimated 600,000 breeding pairs of this relatively common albatross. More than half breed on the Falkland Islands. However, their numbers are declining. They often get entangled in fishing gear and die.

WALRUS

Scientific name: *Odobenus rosmarus*

Location: Arctic Ocean, migrating to sub-Arctic areas in the winter

Walruses on the Pacific Ocean side of the Arctic are larger and 10 times more numerous than those on the Atlantic side. To save them, each Inuit family is allowed to hunt only four a year.

POLAR BEAR

Scientific name: *Ursus marinus*

Location: Coasts and frozen seas of the Arctic and sub-Arctic

Decreasing amounts of Arctic sea ice, where polar bears do their hunting, is likely to drastically affect the future of this flagship species. Experts estimate the world's polar bear numbers at 20,000 to 25,000 at present.

BOWHEAD WHALE

Scientific name: *Balaena mysticetus*

Location: Arctic Ocean, migrating to sub-Arctic seas in the winter

The bowhead is the only large whale to stay in northern waters all year round. This endangered animal was once heavily hunted and populations, especially on the Atlantic side of the Arctic, remain low.

LEOPARD SEAL

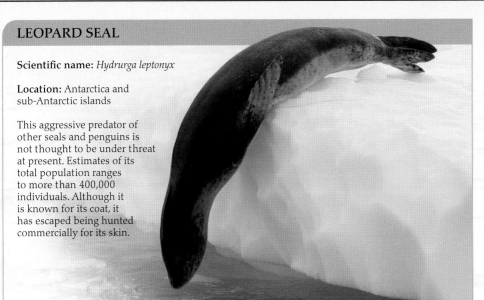

Scientific name: *Hydrurga leptonyx*

Location: Antarctica and sub-Antarctic islands

This aggressive predator of other seals and penguins is not thought to be under threat at present. Estimates of its total population ranges to more than 400,000 individuals. Although it is known for its coat, it has escaped being hunted commercially for its skin.

ARCTIC WOLF

Scientific name: *Canis lupus arctos*

Location: Tundra of Canadian Arctic islands and Greenland

This whitish subspecies of the gray wolf lives in remote regions, where it hunts prey including the muskox. Currently, it is not considered to be a threatened species.

SNOWY OWL

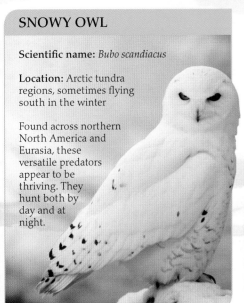

Scientific name: *Bubo scandiacus*

Location: Arctic tundra regions, sometimes flying south in the winter

Found across northern North America and Eurasia, these versatile predators appear to be thriving. They hunt both by day and at night.

BELUGA WHALE

Scientific name: *Delphinapterus leucas*

Location: Arctic and north temperate waters, often among sea ice

Some southerly populations of this widespread species have declined, especially those in Canada's St. Lawrence Estuary, whose health problems may be pollution related.

WOLVERINE

Scientific name: *Gulo gulo*

Location: North America and Eurasia, from Arctic to temperate regions

Wolverines were once trapped extensively for the fur trade. They now survive at low densities throughout many northern forests, mountain areas, and tundra lands.

MUSKOX

Scientific name: *Ovibos moschatus*

Location: Tundra of northern Canada and Greenland (and reintroduced elsewhere)

Today, these hardy cousins of goats and sheep are flourishing and have been reintroduced to Alaska as well as to northern Eurasia, where they last lived thousands of years ago.

Glossary

Siberian husky

ADAPTATION
A feature of a living thing that helps it thrive in its environment and lifestyle. Adaptations are passed on to offspring and evolve over generations.

ANTARCTIC CIRCLE
An imaginary line around Earth toward the South Pole, south of which there is at least one day of 24-hour daylight and 24-hour darkness per year.

ANTARCTIC CONVERGENCE ZONE
A stormy zone in the oceans all around Antarctica, where cold sea water flowing from the Antarctic continent meets and sinks beneath warmer waters lying to the north.

ANTARCTIC PENINSULA
A point of land that stretches northward toward South America on the west side of Antarctica, with milder habitats than the rest of Antarctica.

ARCTIC CIRCLE
An imaginary line around Earth toward the North Pole, north of which there is at least one day of 24-hour daylight and one day of 24-hour darkness per year.

AURORA
Also known as the Northern and Southern lights, flickering lights in the night sky sometimes visible in polar regions, caused by the interaction between high-energy particles from the Sun and Earth's magnetic field.

BERING SEA
A shallow, fertile sea lying south of the Bering Strait connecting the Arctic and the Pacific oceans.

BLUBBER
Fat that forms an insulating layer beneath the skin of whales, seals, and many seabirds.

Icebergs in Jokulsarlon glacier lagoon, Iceland

CARNIVORE
A meat-eating animal; in a narrower sense, a member of the order Carnivora, the mammal group that includes dogs, cats, bears, and seals.

CFCs
Short for chlorofluorocarbons, human-made industrial gases that have been shown to destroy Earth's ozone layer.

COMB JELLY
Transparent jellyfish-like animals that swim in the plankton using rows of beating hairlike structures, called combs.

CORALS
Simple marine animals related to sea anemones. They grow in colonies fixed to a particular spot, supported by a skeleton, and grab their food from the passing water.

CRUSTACEANS
Invertebrate animals with jointed limbs and a hard outer skeleton.

Aurora australis (Southern Lights) at Amundsen–Scott South Pole Station

FALKLAND ISLANDS
Islands in the South Atlantic lying due north of the Antarctic Peninsula, with a milder climate.

GLACIER
A mass of land ice slowly flowing downhill.

GLOBAL WARMING
The current warming trend in the Earth's atmosphere and oceans, thought to be due to increases in greenhouse gases.

GREENHOUSE GAS
Any gas in the atmosphere that tends to absorb heat radiating from Earth's surface, causing the atmosphere to warm up.

HUSKY
A type of dog bred to pull sleds in Arctic areas.

ICE AGE
The alternating series of cold and milder spells that Earth has experienced over the last 2.5 million years, and more specifically, the most recent cold spell ending around 10,000 years ago.

ICE CAP
A mass of permanent land ice similar to an ice sheet but smaller in extent.

ICE FLOE
A drifting section of broken-up sea ice.

ICE SHEET
A very large mass of permanent ice covering land.

ICE SHELF
Ice 100–1,000 m (300–3,000 ft) thick, extending out to sea but attached to land and which begins as ice flowing from an ice sheet.

INUIT
An ethnic group (or members of it) native to northernmost Canada and Greenland whose traditional lifestyle was intricately adapted to surviving in the Arctic environment.

INVERTEBRATE
Any animal without a backbone, including worms, snails, shrimps, starfish, and coral.

KRILL
Shrimplike animals that swim and feed in huge numbers as part of the plankton of polar seas and in turn are food for many larger animals.

LEAD
A channel of open water through sea ice.

LEMMINGS
Small, thick-furred mammals related to voles that are common inhabitants of the Arctic tundra and are important prey for larger animals.

LICHEN
Unique living organism that is an intimate partnership between a fungus and a simple plant (an alga). Small and hardy, lichens can grow as crusts on dry rocks or in leafy or bushy forms, such as the wrongly named reindeer moss.

MAMMAL
A warm-blooded animal, such as humans, dogs, cats, seals, whales, and deer, that suckles its young.

MIGRATION
A regular (usually yearly) large-scale movement of animals of a particular species from one region to another and back again. (A one-way journey, often caused by overcrowding or food shortage, is called an irruption.)

MOLLUSKS
A major group of invertebrate animals that includes snails, slugs, clams, octopuses, and squid, which share the same basic body plan despite their different shapes.

MOSS
Simple low-growing green plant that is nonflowering and lacks stems and roots.

NORTH POLE
The location at which Earth's axis (the imaginary line around which Earth spins) reaches the surface of the Arctic Ocean.

OZONE LAYER
A region high in Earth's atmosphere containing the gas ozone (a form of oxygen) that protects life on Earth from harmful ultraviolet radiation.

PACK ICE
Drifting sea ice, especially when it has been broken up by wave action and then frozen together again.

PEAT
Dead plant material that has accumulated in cool, oxygen-free environments, such as bogs and fens, and as a result has not decayed.

PERMAFROST
Frozen ground found beneath the surface in polar regions. Ground frozen for two or more years continuously can be called permafrost, but some permafrost is thousands of years old.

PLANKTON
Plants or animals living in open water that cannot swim strongly and so drift with the currents. They are usually small or microscopic.

SCAVENGER
An animal that feeds on dead remains, usually of other animals or their food.

SCIENTIFIC NAME
The official name of a species, normally printed in *italic* type. It consists of two words: a genus name written with a capital letter and a species name without one. For example, *Ursus maritimus* is the scientific name of the polar bear.

SEA ICE
Ice that has formed directly on the sea, in contrast to land-formed ice such as an ice shelf or iceberg. It is usually less than 15 ft (5 m) thick.

SEA URCHIN
Rounded, spiny, nonswimming sea animals related to starfish.

SHAMAN
A person in many traditional tribal societies who is regarded as having direct access to the spiritual world, and therefore is able to carry out functions such as curing illnesses and communicating with the dead.

SHELLFISH
A term for marine invertebrates that have hard outer shells, especially mollusks and crustaceans.

SOUTH POLE
The point at which Earth's axis (the imaginary line around which Earth spins) reaches the surface of the Antarctic continent.

SQUID
Fast-swimming marine invertebrates of the open ocean related to octopuses, with two long tentacles and eight shorter arms.

Flock of snow geese in flight during migration

SUB-ANTARCTIC
Relating to regions north of Antarctica where conditions are less severe than in Antarctica itself. The phrase "sub-Antarctic islands" refers to any of the numerous islands dotting the ocean north of Antarctica.

SUB-ARCTIC
Relating to northern regions and habitats that are milder than the Arctic but colder than temperate lands. In marine terms, this includes seas of the north Pacific where there is some ice cover; on land, it refers to regions that have very cold winters but whose summers are warmer than those of the true Arctic.

SVALBARD
A group of Arctic islands north of, and belonging to, Norway. The main island is Spitzbergen.

TEMPERATE
Relating to the regions of Earth with moderate temperatures between the tropics and the polar regions.

THERMAL
Relating to heat or temperature.

TRANSANTARCTIC MOUNTAINS
Longest mountain range in Antarctica, dividing the continent into East and West Antarctica.

TUNDRA
Treeless regions dominated by low-growing, cold-tolerant plants. Tundra is widespread in northern North America and Eurasia.

ULTRAVIOLET
Invisible high-energy light radiated from the Sun that can sometimes damage living things. Much of it is absorbed by Earth's ozone layer.

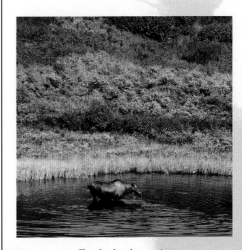

Tundra landscape in Denali National Park, Alaska

Index

Acknowledgments

Dorling Kindersley would like to thank:
Laurence Errington for the index; Monica Byles for proofreading; Caitlin Doyle for Americanization; Open Air Cambridge Ltd. for the use of their clothing and equipment; the staff of Tierpark Dählhölzli, Bern, Switzerland, for their time and trouble; Tony Hall at the Royal Botanical Gardens, Kew; Julia Nicholson and the Pitt Rivers Museum, Oxford; Robert Headland and the staff of the Scott Polar Institute, Cambridge; Whipsnade Zoo, Bedfordshire; The British School of Falconry, Gleneagles, Scotland; Ivan Finnegan, Kati Poynor, Robin Hunter, Manisha Patel, Andrew Nash, Susan St. Louis, and Aude van Ryn for design and illustration assistance.
Additional photography: Lynton Gardiner at the American Museum of Natural History (60/61b); Neil Fletcher (1c); Dave King (37cr); Minden Pictures (42cl); Harry Taylor at the Natural History Museum (45tl, 47tr); University Museum, Cambridge (43cr); Jerry Young (16cl, 17c, 32/33, 40tl) **Maps:** Simon Mumford; Sallie Alane Reason **Model:** Gordon Models

Picture credits
The publisher would like to thank the following for their kind permission to reproduce their photographs:

t=top b=bottom c=center l=left r=right

Aardman Animations: 28cr **Ardea:** 36c; /Jean-Paul Ferrero 28bc; /François Gohier 45cr; /Graham Robertson 30c; **B. & C. Alexander:** 6/7b, 8bl, 11ctr, 15t, 21c, 23c, 25br, 38tl, 39tcr, 42bl, 42/43b, 44bl,

44br, 59c, 60cbl, 61cbr, 62tl, 62tr; /Paul Drummond 23tl; Barnaby's Picture Library /Rothman: 6/7c; Bridgeman Art Library: 25tl; / British Library 7tl; /National Maritime Museum 52cl; **British Antarctic Survey:** 10tr, 12ctl, 23bl; /D.G. Allan 13 tr, 13br; /C.J. Gilbert 10cl, 10bl, 12tl; /E. Jarvis 45br; /B. Thomas 61cr; **Bruce Coleman Ltd.:** 14/15b, 34tl, 35bl, 36bl, 36br; Jen & Des Bartlett 20cl /Roger A. Goggan 12/13; /Johnny Johnson 7tr; /Stephen J. Krasemann 19br; /Len Rue Jr. 40bl; /John Shaw 41c; /Keith Nels Swenson 11ctl; /Rinie van Meurs 29cr; **Corbis:** Richard Baker / In Pictures 67bl; Michael S. Nolan / Terra 6–7b; Radius Images 69br; Denis Scott / Comet 68b; **E.T. Archive:** 6tr; **Getty Images:** Tom Brakefield / Photodisc 71tr; Yvette Cardozo / Workbook Stock 69c; Daniel J. Cox / Photographer's Choice 69bl; Peter Lilja / The Image Bank 64c; Nathalie Michel / The Image Bank 69tl; **Illustrated London News:** 20tl, 26cr; **Frank Lane Picture Agency:** /Hannu Hautala 17tcl; /E. & D. Hosking 22c; /Peter Moore 14cl; /F. Pölking 32cl; /Mark Newman 38c; /Tony Wharton 17tl; **Mary Evans Picture Library:** 8tl, 9tr, 38tr, 40cr, 41tr, 42tl, 46tr, 54bl, 55ct, 55cr, 55bc, 56tl; NASA: 63tl; Goddard Space Flight Center Scientific Visualization Studio 67, 67cr; **Courtesy of the National Science Foundation:** Rhys Boulton 70cl; **Natural History Photographic Agency:** /B. & C. Alexander 10/11; /Melvin Grey 20/21b; /Brian Hawkes 29tl; /Tony Howard /ANT 10c; /E.A. James 29tr; /Peter Johnson 27c; /Stephen Krasemann 37tr; /Lady Philippa Scott 27bl; **Robert Opie Collection:** 59cr; **Oxford Scientific Films:** 27tl; / Doug Allan 12c, 12b, 16bl, 30tl, 44cr; /Michael Brooke 22tl; /S.R. Maglione 14/15t; /Colin Monteath 22b; /S.R. Morris 35cl; /Owen

Newman 20ctl; /Ben Osborne 26bl, 28l, 29b; /Richard Packwood 36tl; /Konrad Wothe 32bcr; **Planet Earth Pictures:** /Gary Bell 33tcl; /Peter Scoones 29tc; /Scott McKinley 9cr; /Bora Merdsoy 13bl; **Royal Geographical Society:** 53cr, 53tr, 56cl; /Alastair Laidlaw 53br; **Science Photo Library:** /Dr. David Millar 63bl; / Claude Nuridsany & Marie Perennou 62cl; **Zefa Picture Library:** / Allstock 31c; /Frans Lanting 26tl

Jacket images: Front: Dorling Kindersley: Jerry Young ca, ftl. **Getty Images:** Frank Krahmer / Photographer's Choice RF (main image). *Back:* **Dorling Kindersley:** The American Museum of Natural History bc; Pitt Rivers Museum, University of Oxford cr.

Wall chart: Bryan & Cherry Alexander / ArcticPhoto: cl/ (walrus); **Dorling Kindersley:** The American Museum of Natural History cr, Gordon Models – modelmaker ftl, Natural History Museum, London fcra; **Getty Images:** Arctic-Images / Iconica fbl/ (tern), Stone / Kevin Schafer bc; **Photolibrary:** Oxford Scientific (OSF) / Doug Allan fbl, cra, Peter Arnold Images / Jonathan Bird tr; **Photoshot:** NHPA / Bryan and Cherry Alexander Photography fcla
All other images © Dorling Kindersley
For further information, see: www.dkimages.com

Every effort has been made to trace the copyright holders. Dorling Kindersley apologizes for any unintentional omissions and would be pleased, in such cases, to add an acknowledgment in future editions.